William Blackstone

A Translation of All the Greek, Latin, Italian, and French Quotations

Quotations

which occur in Blackstone's Commentaries on the laws of England

William Blackstone

A Translation of All the Greek, Latin, Italian, and French Quotations
which occur in Blackstone's Commentaries on the laws of England

ISBN/EAN: 9783337236878

Printed in Europe, USA, Canada, Australia, Japan

Cover: Foto ©Suzi / pixelio.de

More available books at **www.hansebooks.com**

LAW SCHOOL TEXT-BOOKS.

Bills and Notes. By BYLES. Edited by Chief Justice SHARSWOOD. 1 vol. $6 50

Blackstone. A translation of all the Foreign Quotations which occur in Blackstone's Commentaries. By JONES. 1 vol. . . . 1 50

Common Law. BROOM's Commentaries on. 1 vol. . . 6 00

Constitution of the United States. An exposition of. By FLANDERS. Cloth, 1 vol. 1 25

Contracts. By SMITH. Edited by WM. HENRY RAWLE, Chief Justice SHARSWOOD, and J. DOUGLASS BROWN, Jr. 1 vol. . . 5 00

Contracts. Questions and Answers to SMITH. 1 vol. 1 00

Contracts. Discharge of. By RALSTON. 1 vol. . . 1 00

Equity. By ADAMS. Edited by HENRY WHARTON, GEORGE TUCKER BISPHAM, ALFRED I. PHILLIPS, and others. 1 vol. . . 6 50

Evidence. By STARKIE. Edited by Chief Justice SHARSWOOD. 1 vol. 6 50

Law of Nations. By VATTEL. Edited by E. D. INGRAHAM. 1 vol. 3 50

Leading Cases. By SMITH. Edited by HARE and WALLACE. 4 vols. 12 00

Legal Ethics. By Chief Justice SHARSWOOD. Cloth, 1 vol. . . 1 50

Legal Maxims. By BROOM. 1 vol. . . 6 50

Personal Property. By WILLIAMS. 1 vol. 5 00

Personal Property. Questions and Answers to WILLIAMS. 1 vol. 1 00

Real Property. By WILLIAMS. Edited by WM. HENRY RAWLE, Hon. JAS. T. MITCHELL, and Prof. E. COPPÉE MITCHELL. 1 vol. 5 00

Real Property. Questions and Answers to WILLIAMS. 1 vol. 1 00

Roman Law. By MACKELDEY. Edited by DROPSIE. 1 vol. 6 50

Wills, Construction of. By HAWKINS. Edited by F. M. LEONARD. 1 vol. 5 00

STUDENTS' PRICES ON APPLICATION TO,

T. & J. W. JOHNSON & CO.
535 Chestnut Street, Philadelphia, Pa.

A

TRANSLATION

OF ALL THE

GREEK, LATIN, ITALIAN, AND FRENCH QUOTATIONS

WHICH OCCUR IN

BLACKSTONE'S COMMENTARIES

ON THE LAWS OF ENGLAND;

AND ALSO IN

THE NOTES OF THE EDITIONS

BY

CHRISTIAN, ARCHBOLD, AND WILLIAMS.

———

By J. W. JONES, Esq.

LATE OF GRAY'S INN.

———

PHILADELPHIA:

T. & J. W. JOHNSON & CO.

1889.

PREFACE.

IF the excellence of a book be best proved by the universality of its reception, there are few of greater merit than the Commentaries of Blackstone — a work, although expressly treating of the Laws of England, not confined to the library of the lawyer, but occupying a distinguished place in every collection of books bearing in any degree the character of judicious selection.

The mass of information contained in it, not legal only, but historical, and of times where the researches of historians are confessedly involved in darkness, and its consequent doubt, often tends to corroborate facts the truth of which the isolated details of early history leave unascertained, from some chasm in the chain of consequences ill supplied, or inconsistency in the character of the persons or the circumstances connected with their production.

The enactment and repeal of statutes derive their cause and occasion from the vicissitude inherent in the nature of all human affairs — whether resulting from the schemes of avarice, or the progress of ambition — from the emulations of genius, or the transforming powers of persevering industry — from the darkness of superstition, or the light of science — and in the history of them transiently convey such sketches of the form and character of times, persons, and things long past and forgotten, as by no other means can now be known — and the customs and manners of the darker ages are sometimes rendered more clearly obvious by the detached clauses of an old decree than by the most labored deductions from regular history. Of this species of illustration frequent instances occur in the Commentaries of Blackstone — but they are often illustration only to the more learned reader. Many no doubt there are, who in the perusal of his valuable pages find their progress continually impeded by the old law Latin and Norman French left uninterpreted by the author and his editors, and to such, consequently, a large and important portion of the work is mere dead letter. To render it available to this description of its readers, the following version is respectfully offered as a Companion to Blackstone, by the translator,

Nov. 1st, 1823.   J. W. JONES.

ADVERTISEMENT.

The numbers correspond to the marginal paging of the Commentaries. Where Blackstone has given the sense of any passage it has not been translated here.

A

TRANSLATION,

&c., &c.

VOLUME THE FIRST.

ADVERTISEMENT.

XI. Quam peritus ille et privati juris et publici! Quantum rerum, quantum exemplorum, quantum antiquitatis tenet! Nihil est quod discere velis, quod ille docere non potest! Mihi certe, quoties aliquid abditum quaero, ille thesaurus est.

How skillful he is both in public and in private law! What a knowledge he possesses of things, of examples, and of antiquity! There is nothing you would learn which he cannot teach. In every difficulty he is my constant resource.

Placitum—Placita.	Marginal titles.
Ex ordine.	According to their order.

6. Facultas ejus, quod cuique facere libet, nisi quid vi, aut jure, prohibetur.
Its essence is the power of doing whatsoever we please, unless where authority or law forbids.

---

7. Vera lex, recta ratio, naturæ congruens.
True law, right reason, conformable to nature.

---

10. Est senatori, &c. [translated in the text.]

---

12. Turpe esse, &c. [translated in the text.]

---

15. Dedicatio corporis juris civilis. Dedication to the body of civil law.

16. Quia juris civilis studiosos decet haud imperitos esse juris municipalis, et differentias exteri patriique juris notas habere.
For students of civil law should not be ignorant of the municipal law nor of the remarkable differences between their own laws and those of foreign nations.

16. Doctor legum mox a doctoratu dabit operam legibus Angliæ, ut non sit imperitus earum legum quas habet sua patria, et differentias exteri patriique juris noscat.

A doctor of laws, having taken his degree, should study the laws of England, that he be not unskilled in those of his own country, nor be ignorant of the essential differences between them and foreign laws.

17. Nullus clericus nisi causidicus. No clergyman who is not a lawyer also.

---

17. Foro seculari.   In the secular court.

---

17. A fortiori.   By a stronger reason.

---

17. Les juges sont sages personnes et autentiques—sicome les archevesques, evesques, les chanoines des eglises cathedraulx, et les autres personnes qui ont dignitez in saincte eglise; les abbez, les prieurs conventaulx, et les gouverneurs des eglises, &c.

The judges are persons of wisdom and authority—such as archbishops, bishops, canons of cathedral churches, and other dignitaries of holy church, the abbies, priors of convents and church governors, &c.

---

19. Et omnes comites, &c. [translated in the text.]

---

19. Quod principi placuit legis habet vigorem.
The constitution of the prince has the force of law.

---

19. Judicium parium vel lex terræ.
The judgment of the peers or law of the land.

---

20. In foro seculari.   In the secular court.

---

21. Summa de laudibus Christiferæ Virginis (divinum magis quam humanum opus). "Item quod jura civilia, et leges, et decreta scivit in summo, probatur hoc modo; sapientia advocati manifestatur in tribus; unum quod obtineat omnia contra judicem justum et sapientem; secundo, quod contra adversarium astutum et sagacem; tertio, quod in causa desperata: sed beatissima virgo, contra judicem sapientissimum, Dominum; contra adversarium callidissimum, diabolum; in causa nostra desperata; sententiam optatam obtinuit."

Perfections of the Christ-bearing Virgin (a work more divine than human). "Likewise that she had a perfect knowledge of civil rights, laws, and decrees is thus proved:—the wisdom of an advocate is manifested in three things—first, that he have a prevailing influence before a wise and just judge; secondly, against a subtle and sagacious adversary; and thirdly, in a desperate cause: The most blessed Virgin obtained the desired judgment from the most wise judge, the Lord—against our most cunning enemy, the devil—in our desperate cause."

---

21. Nec videtur incongruum mulieres habere peritiam juris. Legitur

enim de uxore Joannis Andreæ glossatoris, quod tantam peritiam in utro-
que jure habuit, ut publice in scholis legere ausa sit.

Nor does a knowledge of the law seem inconsistent with the female
character. For we read that the wife of John Andrew the Lexicographer,
was so skilled both in the common and municipal law, that she ventured
to deliver lectures on both publicly in the schools.

22. Contra inhibitionem novi operis.
Contrary to the prohibition of a new work.

---

22. De novi operis nuntiatione.
Concerning the denunciation of a new work.

---

22. In ceux parolx, "contra inhibitionem novi operis" ny ad pas entend-
ment.
In these words, "contrary to the prohibition of a new work," there
is no meaning.

---

22. Ceo n'est que un restitution en leur ley, pur que a ceo n'avemus
regard, &c.
This is but a restitution in their law, therefore we shall pay no regard to it.

---

23. Aula regis.　　　　　　　In the King's court.

---

23. Pro & con.　　　　　　　For and against.

---

24. Servientis ad legem.　　　Of a serjeant at law.

---

24. Quos banci narratores vulgariter appellamus.
Whom we commonly call bench reporters.

---

24. Voluit ligamenta coiffe suæ solvere ut palam monstraret se tonsuram
habere clericalem; sed non est permissus.—Satelles vero eum arripiens, non
per coiffe ligamina sed per guttur eum apprehendens, traxit ad carcerem.
He wished to untie the strings of his coif that he might prove to all
his having the clerical tonsure; but this was not allowed.—Then an officer
seizing him, not by the strings of his coif but by his throat, dragged him
to prison.

---

24. Ne aliquis scholas, &c. [translated in the text.]

---

25. Passim—Every where—through the whole work.

---

27. Τελεια μαλιστα, &c. [translated in the text.]

---

30. Pomeria.　　　　　　　The bounds.

---

31. Emisit me mater Londinum, juris nostri capessendi gratia; cujus cum

vestibulum salutassem, reperissemque linguam peregrinam, dialectum barbaram, methodum inconcinnam, molem non ingentem solum sed perpetuis humeris sustinendam, excidit mihi (fateor) animus, &c.

My mother sent me to London to commence the study of the law; but when, having paid my respects to the vestibule of this branch of learning I was met by a foreign language, a barbarous dialect, an uncouth style, and a mass not only vast but always to be endured, I confess my courage failed me.

32. Ita lex scripta est.	So the law is written.
32. A priori.	Beforehand.

33. Nisi leguleius quidem cautus, et acutus præco actionum, cantor formularum, auceps syllabarum.

Than a smatterer in law, wary, indeed, and a smart prater about actions, a setter-forth of forms, a captious wrangler.

35. Incipientibus nobis exponere jura populi Romani, ita videntur tradi posse commodissime, si primo levi ac simplici via singula tradantur; alioqui, si statim ab initio rudem adhuc et infirmum animum studiosi multitudine ac varietate rerum oneravimus, duorum alterum, aut desertorem studiorum efficiemus, aut cum magno labore, sæpe etiam cum diffidentia (quæ plerumque juvenes avertit) serius ad id perducemus, ad quod, leviore via ductus, sine magno labore, et sine ulla diffidentia maturius perduci potuisset.

To us about to expound the laws of the Romans, it seems that it may be done more advantageously if first delivered separately and in an easy and simple manner; otherwise, if in the very beginning we burden the mind of the student, as yet unexercised and weak, with a multitude and diversity of things, we either cause him to relinquish his studies altogether, or bring him much later, with great labor, and often with great diffidence (which very frequently deters young men) to that point, to which, conducted by a more easy method, he might have been brought earlier, with little trouble, and with sufficient confidence.

39. Γενεσθω φως και εγενετο.	Let there be light and there was light.
40. Suum cuique tribuere.	To give to everyone his due.

40. Juris præcepta sunt hæc, honeste vivere, alterum non lædere, suum cuique tribuere.

The precepts of the law are these, to live honestly, not to injure another, and to give to every one his due.

41. Jura naturæ sunt immutabilia.	The laws of nature are immutable.
41. Leges legum.	The laws of laws.

42. Melius est omnia mala pati quam malo consentire.
It is better to endure every evil than to consent to evil.

---

42. Malum in se.   Crime in itself.

---

42. Corruptela.   A mere mischief.

---

43. In foro conscientiæ.   In the court of conscience.

---

43. Quod naturalis ratio inter omnes homines constituit, vocatur jus gentium.
That rule which natural reason has dictated to all men, is called the law of nations.

---

44. Jus civile est quod quisque sibi populus constituit.
The civil law is that which every nation has established for its own government.

---

44. Quod quisque populus ipse sibi jus constituit, id ipsius proprium civitatis est, vocaturque jus civile, quasi jus proprium ipsius civitatis.
That which a people have decreed as law for themselves is peculiar to that city or nation, and is called the civil law, as being the law of that particular country.

---

44. Lex est summa ratio insita a natura quæ jubet ea, quæ facienda sunt, prohibetque contraria.
Law is the perfection of reason implanted in us by nature, which enjoins what should be done, and forbids what we should not do.

---

45. Viva voce.   By word of mouth.

---

46. Ex post facto.   After the fact.

---

46. In futuro.   At a future period.

---

46. Privilegia.   Private laws.

---

46. Vetant leges sacratæ, vetant duodecim tabulæ, leges privatis hominibus irrogari; id enim est privilegium. Nemo unquam tulit: nihil est crudelius, nihil perniciosius, nihil quod minus hæc civitas ferre possit.
The sacred laws forbid, the twelve tables forbid, that the interests of private individuals should be affected by special laws; for that is privilege. There has never been an instance of it: nothing could be more cruel, nothing more injurious, nothing which to this nation could be less tolerable.

---

50. Esse optime constitutam rempublicam, quæ ex tribus generibus illis, regali, optimo, et populari, sit modice confusa.
That the best constituted republic, is that which is duly compounded of these three estates, the monarchical, aristocratical, and democratical.

50. Cunctas nationes et urbes, populus, aut primores, aut singuli regunt: delecta ex his et constituta reipublicæ forma laudari facilius quam eveniri, vel, si evenit, haud diuturna esse potest.

The government of all cities or countries is either democratical, aristocratical, or monarchical. It is more easy to approve of a government composed of these three in the form of a republic than to carry it into execution; or if effected, it cannot be lasting.

51. Principium et fons.	The origin and source.
54. Mala in se.	Crimes in themselves.
57. Mala prohibita.	Crimes, because forbidden.

58. Atque ipsa utilitas justi prope mater et æqui.

Utility itself may be said to be the parent of all that is lawful and equitable.

58. Juris positivi.	Of positive law.
58. Omnia peccata sunt paria.	All offences are equal.

58. Lex pure pœnalis obligat tantum ad pœnam, non item ad culpam: lex pœnalis mixta et ad culpam obligat et ad pœnam.

The object of a law purely penal regards the punishment solely, not the crime also: a mixed penal law involves both the crime and punishment.

62. Lex non exacte definit, sed arbitrio boni viri permittit.

The law does not define exactly, but leaves something to the discretion of a just and wise judge.

62. Summum jus.	The rigor of the law.
62. Summa injuria.	The highest injury.

63. Leges sola memoria et usu retinebant.

They retained their laws solely by memory and custom.

64. Tacito et illiterato hominum consensu et moribus expressum.

Expressed or sanctioned by the tacit and unwritten customs and consent of men.

65. Omnibus qui reipublicæ præsunt etiam atque etiam mando, ut omnibus æquos se præbeant judices, perinde ac in judiciali libro scriptum habetur; nec quicquam formident quin jus commune audacter libereque dicant.

To all who preside over the republic, my positive and repeated injunction is, that they conduct themselves towards all as just judges, as it is written in the dome-book, and without fear boldly and freely to declare the common law.

66. Lex Angliæ.   The law of England.

66. Lex terræ.   The law of the land.

66. Legum Anglicanarum conditor.   The founder of the English laws.

66. Restitutor.   The restorer.

69. Viginti annorum lucubrationes. The lucubrations of twenty years.

69. Præteritorum memoria eventorum. The remembrance of past events.

69. Legibus patriæ optime instituti.
Best instructed in the laws of their country.

70. Jus dicere   To declare the law.

70. Jus dare.   To enact the law.

70. Argumentum ab inconvenienti plurimum valet in lege.
The plea of inconvenience is, in law, the most weighty.

70. Nihil quod est inconveniens est licitum.
Nothing which is inconvenient is lawful.

70. Non omnium, quæ a majoribus nostris constituta sunt, ratio reddi potest; et ideo rationes eorum quæ constituuntur inquiri non oportet; alioquin multa ex his quæ certa sunt subvertuntur.
Reasons cannot be given for all the laws which our ancestors have appointed; therefore we should not seek them; otherwise many of those laws which are established would be subverted.

71. Si imperialis majestas causam cognitionaliter examinaverit, et partibus, cominus constitutis, sententiam dixerit, omnes omnino judices, qui sub nostro imperio sunt, sciant hanc esse legem, non solum illi causæ pro qua producta est, sed et in omnibus similibus.
If the Emperor shall have examined the cause, and shall immediately declare his opinion, let all the judges of the land know that this is law, not only with respect to that cause which first produced the opinion, but to every other of the like nature.

72. Κατ' εξοχην.   By way of pre-eminence.

74. Quod principi placuit legis habet vigorem, cum populus ei et in eum omne suum imperium et potestatem conferat.

The constitution of the prince has the force of law, as the people place all their power and authority in his hands.

74. Imperator solus et conditor et interpres legis existimatur.

The Emperor alone is considered both as the maker and interpreter of the law.

74. Sacrilegii instar est rescripto principis obviari.

It is sacrilege to oppose the rescript of the prince.

74.   CONSTITUTIO.

Sed et quod principi placuit legis habet vigorem: quum lege regia, quæ de ejus imperio lata est populus ei, et in eum omne suum imperium et potestatem concedat. Quodcumque ergo imperator per epistolam constituit; vel cognoscens decrevit, vel edicto præcipit, legem esse constat; hæc sunt quæ constitutiones appellantur. Plane ex his quædam sunt personales, quæ nec ad exemplum trahuntur, quoniam non hoc princeps vult, nam quod alicui ob meritum indulsit, vel si quam pœnam irrogavit, vel si cui sine exemplo subvenit, personam non transgreditur. Aliæ, autem, quum generales sint, omnes procul dubio tenent.

CONSTITUTION.

But also the constitution of the prince has the force of law: as by a law called the LEX REGIA, the people yield all their authority and power to him. It is evident, therefore, that whatever the Emperor has appointed by rescript, decreed as a judge, or ordained by edict, is law; these are what are called constitutions. Of these some are personal, which are not brought forward as precedents, the Prince not willing it; for what he has conferred as matter of grace, or reward, or inflicted as punishment, or granted as unprecedented indulgence, does not extend beyond the particular object of it. But what is general, is doubtless binding on all.

74. Sine scripto jus venit, quod usus approbavit, nam diuturni mores consensu utentium comprobati legem imitantur.

Writing is not necessary to make that law which custom has rendered binding; for customs of long duration, sanctioned by common consent, resemble or stand in the place of law.

74. Vi et armis.   By force and arms.

75. Cuilibet in sua arte credendum est.
Every man is to be credited in what concerns his own profession.

75. Lex et consuetudo parliamenti.   The law and custom of parliament.

76. Malus usus abolendus est.   A bad custom should be abolished.

78. Id certum est quod certum reddi potest.
That is certain which can be made certain.

79. Leges non scriptæ. Unwritten laws.

---

80. Tam immensus aliarum super alias acervatarum legum cumulus.
Such a vast pile of laws heaped one upon the other.

---

81. Corpus juris civilis. The body of civil law.

---

81. Senatus Consulta. Acts of the Senate.

---

81. Plebiscita. Decrees of the people without the Senate.

---

81. Edictum perpetuum. A perpetual edict.

---

82. Concordia discordantium canonum.
The arrangement of the confused canons

---

82. Decretum Gratiani. The decree of Gratian.

---

82. Decretalia Gregorii noni. The decretals of Gregory the ninth.

---

82. Sextus decretalium. A sixth decretal.

---

82. Extravagantes Joannis. The extravagants of John.

---

82. Extravagantes Communes. Common Extravagants.

---

82. E vedi in tanto le strane vicende delle mondane cose: questa grand'
opera di Giustiniano con tanta cura, e studio compilata, che per tutti i secoli
avrebbe dovuto correre gloriosa, e immortale, appena mancato il suo autore,
che restò anch' ella per lo spazio di cinque secoli sepolta in tenebre densissime,
ed in una profonda oblivione; risorta poi in occidente a tempi di Lottario,
fu così avventurosa, che alzò i vanni e la fama sopra tutte l'altre provincie
del mondo, ne trovo nazione alcuna culta, o barbara, che fosse, che in somma
stima, e venerazione non l'avesse, e che non la preferisse alle medesime
loro proprie leggi, e costumi.

How strange are the vicissitudes of worldly things! This great work
of Justinian, compiled with so much care and study, that it was worthy to
be handed down from age to age with immortal honor; scarcely was its
author dead, than even this great work remained buried—lost to the world
during the course of five hundred years, in profound oblivion. It was afterwards restored to light in the west, in the reign of Lothario, under such
fortunate auspices, that its fame spread through the world, nor was there
any nation, whether barbarous or civilized, which did not hold it in the highest esteem and veneration, and prefer it even to its own laws and customs.

---

84. Leges sub graviori lege. Laws subject to a more weighty law.

---

85. Articuli cleri. The articles of the clergy.

85.	Prerogativa regis.	The King's prerogative.
85.	Quia emptores.	Because purchasers.
85.	Circumspecte agatis.	That ye act circumspectly.
86.	Ex officio.	In the course of duty: by virtue of office.
86.	Senatus decreta.	Decrees of the Senate.
86.	Senatus consulta.	Acts of the Senate.

86. In perpetuum rei testimonium. As a lasting testimony of the thing.

89. Ut res magis valeat quam pereat.
That the whole subject matter may rather operate than be annulled.

89. Leges posteriores priores contrarias abrogant.
New laws repeal those preceding which are contrary to them.

89. Quod populus postremum jussit id jus ratum esto.
Let that which the people have last decreed be considered as law.

89.	De facto.	In fact.
91.	Quoad hoc.	As to this.

91. Cum lex, &c. [translated in the text.]

94. Terra Walliæ cum incolis suis, prius regi jure feodali subjecta, jam in proprietatis dominium totaliter et cum integritate conversa est, et coronæ regni Angliæ tanquam pars corporis ejusdem annexa et unita.

The country of Wales, together with its inhabitants, was formerly held under the King by the feudal law; it is now completely converted into a principality, and annexed to, and united with, the crown of England, as forming a part of the same kingdom.

94.	Statutum Walliæ	The statute of Wales.
94.	Apud Rothelanum.	At Rhuydland.

94. Terra Walliæ prius regi jure feodali subjecta.
The land of Wales was before subjected to the King by the feudal law.

96. Nihil ratum esse, nihil legis vim habere, nisi quod omnium trium ordinum consensu conjuncto constitutum est; ita tamen ut unius cujusque ordinis per se major pars consentiens pro toto ordine sufficiat. Scio hodie controverti, an duo ordines dissentiente tertio, quasi major pars leges con-

dere possint; cujus partem negantem boni omnes, et quicunque de hac re scripserunt pertinacissime tuentur, alioque duo ordines in eversionem tertii possint consentire.

That nothing is established, nothing has the force of law but what is constituted by the joint consent of all the three estates; the consent of the majority of each being considered as the consent of the whole. I know it is in the present day disputed, whether two of the three estates, the third dissenting, can enact laws as a majority; all just and learned men, and all those who have written on the subject, have pertinaciously defended the party denying the power, arguing that otherwise any two of the orders might agree together to the entire subversion of the third.

99.	Mandamus.	We command.
99.	Habeas corpus.	That you have the body.
99.	Certiorari.	To have notice given him.

100. Pro eo quod leges quibus utuntur Hybernici Deo detestabiles existunt, et omni jure dissonant, adeo quod leges censeri non debeant—nobis et consilio nostro satis videtur expediens, eisdem utendas concedere leges Anglicanas.

Inasmuch as the laws by which the Irish are governed, are hateful to God and incompatible with justice, and therefore ought not to be considered as laws—it seems highly expedient to us and to our council, to give them the laws of England for their government.

110. Divisum imperium.	A divided authority.
111. Paroichia.	Parishes.

112. Dentur omnes decimae primariae ecclesiae ad quam parochia pertinet.

That all tithes be given to the mother church to which the parish belongs.

114. Summa et maxima securitas, per quam omnes statu firmissimo sustinentur; quae hoc modo fiebat, quod sub decennali fidejussione debebant esse universi.

The best and greatest security by which all persons are kept in the safest state; which was effected in this manner, that every ten should be sureties for each other.

114. Volumus itaque et per presentes ordinamus quod ecclesia cathedralis et sedes episcopales ac quod tota villa nostra Westmonasterii sit civitas ipsamque civitatem Westmonasterii vocari et nominari volumus et decernimus.

We, therefore, will and ordain by these presents, that the Cathedral, and Bishop's see, and our whole town of Westminster become a city, and that it be named and called the city of Westminster.

114. Civitas.   A city.

114. Almæ matri academiæ Cantabrigiæ.
To his alma mater the university of Cambridge.

115. Concessum est episcopis de villis transire in civitates.
It is granted to bishops with respect to their towns that they become
cities.

115. Et quod Angli vocant hundredum, comitatus Yorkshire, Lincolnshire, Nottinghamshire, Leicestershire, et Northamptonshire vocant wap-
pentachium.
And that which the English call a hundred, the counties of Yorkshire, Lincolnshire, Nottinghamshire, Leicestershire, and Northamptonshire call a wappentake.

115. Centenarius.   Head of a hundred.

116. Centeni ex singulis pagis sunt, idque ipsum inter suos vocantur; et
quod primo numerus fuit, jam nomen et honor est.
Each village is divided into hundreds, and are so called by their
inhabitants; and that which first was a mere number has now become both
a name and an honor.

117. A palatio.   From a royal court.

117. Jura regalia.   Regal rights.

117. Regalem potestatem in omnibus.   Regal power in all things.

117. Contra pacem domini Regis.   Against the peace of our lord the King.

117. Contra pacem domini.   Against the peace of the King.

117. Contra pacem ballivorum.   Against the peace of the bailiffs.

117. Contra pacem vice-comitis.   Against the peace of the sheriff.

125. Facultas ejus, &c. [Vide ante, p. 6.]

127.   Fallitur egregie quisquis sub principe credit
               Servitium. Nunquam libertas gratior extat
               Quam sub rege pio.
Whosoever supposes it slavery to live under a prince is greatly de-
ceived. Never does liberty exist more freely than under a pious king.

127. Κατ' ἐξοχήν.   By way of pre-eminence.

127. Gothones regnantur paulo jam adductius, quam cæteræ Germanorum

gentes, nondum tamen supra libertatem.

The Goths are now governed by a mode rather more strict than the other German tribes, but yet not so as to encroach on the limits of due liberty.

---

127. Falso libertatis vocabulum obtendi ab iis qui privatim degeneres, in publicum exitiosi, nihil spei, nisi per discordias habeant.

The word liberty falsely used as a cover by those who, dishonorable in their private, and dangerous in their public conduct, have no hope but in discord and contention.

---

127. Hanc retinete, quæso Quirites, quam vobis, tanquam hereditatem, majores vestri reliquerunt.

Preserve, I beseech ye, O Romans, this liberty, which your ancestors have left ye as an inheritance.

---

128. Confirmatio chartarum.   A confirmation of the charters.

---

129. Residuum.   The remainder.

---

129. Si aliquis mulierem pregnantem percusserit, vel ei venenum dederit, per quod fecerit abortivam, si puerperium jam formatum fuerit, et maxime si fuerit animatum, facit homicidium.

If any one strike a woman when pregnant, or administer poison to her, by which abortion shall ensue, if the child should be already formed, and particularly if it be alive, that person is guilty of manslaughter.

---

130. Qui in utero sunt, in jure civili intelliguntur in rerum natura esse, cum de eorum commodo agatur.

Those who are in the womb, are considered by the civil law to be in the nature of things, as they are capable of being benefited.

---

130. Se defendendo.   In self-defence.

---

131. Per minas.   By threats.

---

131. Non suspicio cujuslibet vani et meticulosi hominis, sed talis qui possit cadere in virum constantem; talis enim debet esse metus, qui in se contineat vitæ periculum, aut corporis cruciatum.

It must not be the apprehension of a foolish and fearful man, but such as a courageous man may be susceptible of; it should be, for instance, such a fear as consists in an apprehension of bodily pain, or danger to life.

---

131. Ignoscitur ei qui sanguinem suum qualiter redemptum voluit.

He is justified who has acted in pure defence of his own life or limb.

---

132. Desiit esse miles seculi qui factus est miles Christi, nec beneficium pertinet ad eum qui non debet gerere officium.

He who becomes a soldier of Christ hath ceased to be a soldier of the world, nor is he entitled to any reward who acknowledges no duty.

132. Civiliter mortuus.   Dead in law.

133. Nullus liber homo aliquo modo destruatur nisi per legale judicium parium suorum, aut per legem terræ.

No freeman shall be deprived of life but by the lawful judgment of his peers, or by the law of the land.

135. Lettres de cachet.

Letters of the Signet—A power assumed by the Kings of France, of arresting any person without giving a reason for the procedure.

135. Unigenitus.   The only-begotten.

136. Dent operam consules ne quid respublica detrimenti capiat.

Let the consuls take care that the commonwealth receive no injury.

136. Senatus consultum ultimæ necessitatis.

The decree of the Senate on emergencies of especial consequence.

137. Ne exeat regno.   Let him not leave the kingdom.

138. Præmunire. To forewarn. [Vide Commentaries, vol. iv., p. 103.]

140. De talliagio non concedendo. Concerning the not granting talliage.

140. Confirmatio Cartarum.   A confirmation of the charters.

141. Nulli vendemus, nulli negabimus, nulli differemus rectum vel justitiam.

To none will we sell, to none deny, to none delay either right or justice.

141. In bonis, in terris, vel persona. Either in his goods, lands, or person.

145. Esto perpetua.   Mayst thou endure forever.

147. Parler le ment.   To speak the mind.

147. Johannes Rex haud dicam Parliamentum, nam hoc nomen non tum emicuit, sed communis consilii regni formam et coactionem perspicuam dedit.

I cannot say that King John ordained the Parliament, for that name was not then used, but he appointed the form and open assembling of the common council of the kingdom.

147. Modus tenendi Parliamentum tempore regis Edwardi, filii regis Etheldredi.

The manner of holding the Parliament in the time of King Edward son of Etheldred.

---

147. De minoribus rebus principes consultant, de majoribus omnes.
The princes consult concerning matters of small consequence, in greater matters the whole nation.

147. Parium lamentum.	A lamentation of the peers.

---

147. Testari mentem.	To declare his mind.

---

148. Commune consilium regni, magnum consilium regis, curia magna, conventus magnatum vel procerum, assisa generalis.
The common council of the kingdom, the great council of the king, the high court, the assembly of the nobles, and the general assize.

148. Commune concilium.	The common council.

---

148. Allodia.	Free lands.

---

148. Beneficia.	Benefices.

---

148. Communitas regni Angliæ. The community of the kingdom of England.

148. Novis injuriis emersis nova constituere remedia.
New injuries having arisen, to appoint new remedies for them.

---

148. Hæc sunt instituta quæ Edgarus Rex consilio sapientum suorum instituit.
These are the laws which King Edgar has instituted in an assembly of the wise men of his realm.

---

148. Hæc sunt judicia quæ sapientes consilio regis Ethelstani instituerunt.
These are the decrees which the wise men, with the advice of King Ethelstane, have appointed.

---

148. Hæc sunt institutiones, quas Rex Edmundus et episcopi sui cum sapientibus suis instituerunt.
These are the institutions which King Edmund and his bishops and his wise men have decreed.

---

148. Quanta esse, &c. [translated in the text.]

---

150. Faciemus summoneri, &c. ad certum diem, scilicet ad terminum quadraginta dierum ad minus et ad certum locum.
We will cause to be summoned, &c. at a certain day, that is within forty days at the least, and at a certain place.

152. Ex necessitate rei.   From the urgency of the affair.

153. Universæ personæ regni.   Every man in the kingdom.

153. In capite.   In chief, or of the king.

153. Que plese a nre dit Sr de tenir parlement un foetz par an au meynz, et ceo en lieu convenable.

That it please our said Lord to hold a parliament once a year at least, and in some convenient place.

153. Caput, principium et finis.   The head, beginning, and end.

154. Sulla tribunis plebis sua lege injuriæ faciendæ potestatem ademit, auxilii ferendi reliquit.

Sulla, by his law, deprived the tribunes of the people of the power of doing injury, but left them that of protection.

159. De communi consilio super negotiis quibusdam arduis et urgentibus, regem, statum, et defensionem regni Angliæ et ecclesiæ Anglicanæ concernentibus.

Concerning the common council upon certain difficult and urgent affairs relating to the king, the state, and defence of the kingdom of England and of the English church.

160. Si antiquitatem spectes, est vetustissima; si dignitatem, est honoratissima; si jurisdictionem, est capacissima.

If you consider its antiquity, it is most antient; if its dignity, it is most honorable; if its jurisdiction, it is most extensive.

161. Potentiores ad laborandum.   The ablest to labor.

163. Lex et consuetudo parliamenti.   The law and custom of parliament.

163. Ab omnibus quærenda, a multis ignorata, a paucis cognita.
To be sought by all, unknown to many, known by few.

163. Lex parliamenti est a multis ignorata.
Many are ignorant of the law of parliament.

164. Ex post facto.   After the fact.

165. Ad synodos venientibus, sive summoniti sint, sive per se quid agendum habuerint, sit summa pax.

Let there be perfect security to those coming to the synods; whether summoned or coming on their own business.

165. Extenditur hæc pax et securitas ad quatuordecim dies, convocato regni senatu.

This freedom from molestation is extended to fourteen days from the assembling of the senate of the kingdom.

---

166. Supersedeas.
That you forbear.— A command to stay or forbear doing that which ought not to be done.

---

166. Ab initio.   From the beginning.

---

166. Contra pacem domini regis.   Against the king's peace.

---

168. Ad tractandum et consilium impendendum.
For consulting and giving advice.

---

168. Ad consentiendum.   For consenting.

---

168. Ex licentia regis.   By permission of the king—or royal licence.

---

168. Litera attornatus ad Parliamentum.
By letter of attorney to Parliament.

---

168. Procurator.   A proctor.

---

174. Pro re nata.   According to circumstances.

---

174.   —— pudet hæc opprobria nobis
Et potuisse dici et non potuisse refelli.
We are ashamed of these things not only that they can be said of us, but because the assertion of them cannot be refuted.

---

174. De expensis militum, civium, et burgensium.
Concerning the expenses of the soldiers, citizens, and burgesses.

---

174. Qui sentit commodum debet sentire et onus.
He who derives the advantage ought also to bear the charge.

---

174. Rationabiles expensas suas in veniendo ad dictum Parliamentum, ibidem morando, et exinde ad propria redeundo.
Their reasonable expenses in coming to the said parliament, during their attendance there, and for their return home.

---

174. Non sunt aliquæ civitates seu burgi infra comitatum Lancastriæ, de quibus aliqui cives vel burgenses ad dictum Parliamentum venire debent seu solent, nec possunt propter eorum debilitatem et paupertatem.
There are no cities nor boroughs within the county of Lancaster, from which any citizens or burgesses either ought or are accustomed to attend the said Parliament, nor can they on account of their poverty and decay.

175. Nec debet dici tendere in prejudicium ecclesiasticæ libertatis, quod pro rege et republica necessarium invenitur.

Nor should that which is found necessary for the king and commonwealth be considered as tending to the prejudice of ecclesiastical liberty.

175. Pro rege et republica necessarium.

Necessary for the king and commonwealth.

175. Le noun de cellui, qui bailla as ditz communes la dite bille.

The name of him who delivered to the said commons the said bill.

175. Thomas Comes Marescallus et Nottinghamiæ, Capitaneus villæ regis Calesii, qui in obsequio regis in partibus Picardiæ super salva custodia ejusdem villæ moratur, habet literas regis de generali attornatu, sub nominibus Willielmi Bagot chevalier, et Thomas Haxey clerici, per unum annum duraturas.

Teste rege apud Calesium tertio die Octobris. Cancellarius recepit attornatum.

Thomas Earl Marshal and of Nottingham, Governor of the king's town of Calais, who, in the king's service, resideth in Picardy for the safe custody of the same town, hath the king's letter of general attorney under the names of William Bagot, knight, and Thomas Haxey, clerk, to be in force for one year.

Witness the King at Calais, the third day of October. The Chancellor received the attorney.

176. E converso.   On the other hand.

176. De militibus.   Of soldiers.

176. Dum se bene gesserint.

While they shall have conducted themselves well.

176. E contra.   On the other hand.

178. Et pur ceo que elections deivent estres franches, le roi defende sur sa greve forfaiture, que nul haut homme n'autre per poiar des armes, ne per menaces, ne distourbe de faire franche election.

And therefore that elections may be free, the king forbids, under penalty of heavy forfeiture, that any nobleman or other person, should, by force of arms, or by threats, prevent a free election being made.

179. Teste.   Witness.

179. De ambitu.   Of bribery.

181. Chivalier, qui avoit les parolles des communes en cest Parlement.

Knight, who was the Speaker of the Commons in this Parliament.

181. Germanus frater domini Burgavenny, qui electus prolocutor per communes sacræ regiæ majestati est presentatus, et ita egregie, eleganter, prudenter, et diserte in negotio sibi commisso se gessit ut omnium præsentium plausu et lætitia maximam sibi laudem comparavit, cujus laudi sacra regia majestas non modicum eximium honoris cumulum adjecit: nam, præsentibus et videntibus dominis spiritualibus et temporalibus et regni communibus, cum equitis aurati honore et dignitate ad laudem Dei et Sancti Georgii insignivit, quod nemini mortalium per ulla ante sæcula contigisse audivimus.

The brother of Lord Abergavenny, who, being chosen Speaker by the Commons, was presented to his sacred Majesty, and acted so correctly, courteously, prudently, and eloquently in the business entrusted to him, that he received the greatest applause and commendation from all present, to which praise the King made a great and unparalleled addition: for in the presence of the Lords spiritual and temporal, and the Commons of the kingdom, he conferred on him the honor and dignity of knighthood, to the praise of God and St. George, which we have never heard that any one ever before attained under such circumstances.

---

181. Semper presumitur pro negante.
The presumption is always in favor of the defendant.

---

182. Articuli cleri.	Articles of the clergy.

---

182. Via prescriptionis.	By way of prescription.

---

184. Sub silentio.	Tacitly, or in silence.

---

184. Mutatis mutandis.
The respective differences being allowed for—or, being altered according to the circumstances of the case.

---

184. Curia advisare vult.	The court will consider it.

---

184. Quant aut ceste article, il demande grand avisement, et partant le roi se ent avisera par son conseil.
As to this article it requires great consideration, and therefore the King will consult his council upon it.

---

185. Ut statuta illa, et omnes articulos in eisdem contentos, in singulis locis ubi expedire viderit, publice proclamari, et firmiter teneri et observari faciat.
That he cause those statutes, and all articles therein contained, to be publicly proclaimed and strictly observed and kept in every place where it shall seem expedient.

---

186. De novo.	Anew.

---

191. Jure divino.	By divine right.

194. Solent fœminarum ductu bellare, et sexum in imperiis non discernere.

They are accustomed to wage war under the conduct of women, and not to consider sex in the government of their empire.

195. Vice versa.	By converse position.
196. Eo instanti.	From that instant.
196. Hæres natus.	The heir born.
196. Hæres factus.	The heir appointed.
196. Interregnum.	The space between two reigns.

199. Edmundus autem latusferreum, rex naturalis de stirpe regum, genuit Edwardum, et Edwardus genuit Edgarum, cui de jure debebatur regnum Anglorum.

But Edmund Ironside, who was natural king by descent from the race of kings, begat Edward, and Edward begat Edgar, to whom of right the kingdom of England belonged.

199. Absque generali, senatus et populi, conventu et edicto.

Without the general assembly and edict of the senate and people.

200. Dernier resort.	The last resort.

200. Ego Stephanus Dei gratia, assensu cleri et populi in regem Anglorum electus.

I, Stephen, elected King of England, by the grace of God, and the assent of the clergy and people.

201. Regni Angliæ; quod nobis jure competit hæreditario.

Of the kingdom of England; which falls to us by hereditary right.

203. Soit mys, &c. [translated in the text.]

204. De jure.	By right.
204. De facto.	In fact.

204. Nuper de facto, et non de jure, reges Angliæ.

Late kings of England in fact and not of right.

205. Excepta dignitate regali.	The royal dignity being excepted.

218. Piissima regina conjux divi Imperatoris.

The most pious Queen Consort of the sacred Emperor.

218. Circa ardua regni.	Concerning the arduous affairs of the kingdom.

219. Augusta legibus soluta non est.
The Queen is not exempt from the laws.

---

221. Bedefordscire maner. Lestone redd. per annum xxii lib. &c.; ad opus Reginæ ii uncias auri.—Herefordscire: In Lene, &c. consuetud. ut præpositus manerii veniente domina sua (Regina) in maner. præsentaret ei xviii oras denar. ut esset ipsa læto animo.

Bedfordshire: The manor of Leighton pays twenty-two pounds per annum, &c.; two ounces of gold for the Queen's use. Herefordshire: In Lene, &c. it is the custom for the steward of the manor, on the arrival of his lady (the Queen) at the manor to congratulate her with a present of eighteen oras denarii.

---

221. Causa coadunandi, &c. Civitas Lundon, &c. Vicecomes Berkescire, &c. Pro roba, &c. [translated in the text.]

---

221. Solere aiunt barbaros reges Persarum ac Syrorum uxoribus civitates attribuere, hoc modo; hæc civitas mulieri redimiculum præbeat, hæc in collum, hæc in crines, &c.

They say that the barbarian kings of Persia and Syria were accustomed to assess cities for their wives in this manner; one city was to provide her head-dress, another the ornaments for her neck, and the third those for her hair, &c.

---

222. De sturgione observetur, quod rex illum habebit integrum: de balena vero sufficit, si rex habeat caput, et regina caudam.

Of the sturgeon be it known that the king shall have the whole: but with respect to a whale it is sufficient if the king have the head and the queen the tail.

---

223. Pro dignitate regali.   For the royal dignity.

---

224. Primogenitus.   First born.

---

224. Que les fitz eisnes des rois d'Engleterre, c'est assavoir, ceux qui serroient heirs proscheins du roialme d'Engleterre, fuissent Ducs de Cornewaile.

That the eldest sons of the kings of England, that is to say, those who are the next heirs to the crown, should be Dukes of Cornwall.

---

224. Filii primogeniti regum Angliæ primo nativitatis suæ die majoris atque perfectæ præsumuntur ætatis, sic quod liberationem dicti ducatus eo tunc a nobis petere valeant atque de jure obtinere debeant, ac si viginti et unius annorum ætatis plenæ fuissent.

The first born sons of the Kings of England are considered on the very day of their birth to have arrived at full age, so that they may demand from us at that time a release of the said duchy, and obtain it by right, as if they were of the full age of twenty-one years.

---

224. Per ipsum regem et totum consilium in Parliamento.

By the king himself, and the whole council in Parliament.

226. Ex parte paterna.   By the father's side.

227. Consules, a consulendo; reges enim tales sibi associant ad consulendum
Counsellors, from consulting; for kings assemble such for consultation.

227. Ad consulendum, ad defendendum regem.
For advising and defending the king.

229. Secundum subjectam materiam.   According to the subject matter.

230. Virtute officii.   By virtue of their office.

230. Durante beneplacito.   During pleasure.

230. In anno septimo regis Johannis. In the seventh year of King John.

230. Dormivit tamen hoc officium regnante magna Elizabetha.
Nevertheless this office lay dormant during the reign of the great
Elizabeth.

232. In personam.   In respect to the person.

232. In rem.   In respect to the thing.

233. Nec regibus infinita aut libera potestas.
The power of kings should be neither free nor unlimited.

236. Penes me.   In my possession.

236. Ceo est le serement que le roy jurre a soun coronement: que il
gardera et meintenera lez droitez et lez franchisez de seynt esglise grauntez
auncienment dez droitez roys christiens d'Engletere, et quil gardera toutez
sez terrez, honoures et dignites droiturelx et franks del coron du roialme
d'Engletere en tout maner denticrte sanz null maner damenusement, et lez
droitez dispergez dilapidez ou perduz de la corone a soun poiair reappeller
en launcien estate, et quil gardera le peas de seynt esglise et al clergie et al
people de bon accorde, et quil face faire en toutez sez jugementez owel et
droit justice one discretion et misericorde, et quil grauntera a tenure lez
leyes et custumez du roialme, et a soun poiar lez face garder et affirmer que
lez gentez du people avont faitez et estiez, et les malveys leyz et custumes
de tout oustera, et ferme peas et establie al people de soun roialme en ceo
garde esgardera a soun poiair; come Dieu luy aide.
    This is the oath which the king swears at his coronation; that he
will keep and maintain the rights and franchises of holy church granted
anciently by the rightful christian kings of England, and that he will keep
all the lands, honors and dignities, rights and privileges, of the crown of

the kingdom of England in all respects entire, without any kind of injury, and that he will recall to their ancient state, as far as in him lies, all the scattered, injured, or lost rights of the crown, and that he will keep the peace of holy church, and concord between the clergy and people; and that he will cause equal and true justice to be administered in all his judgments with discretion and mercy, and that he will cause to be maintained the laws and customs of the kingdom, and as far as in him lies will make those be confirmed and kept which the people have made and chosen, and will abolish entirely all bad laws and customs, and will, in all respects, as far as he can, maintain a firm and established peace for the people of his kingdom: So help him God.

237. Arcana imperii.   The secrets of the empire.

237. Bona Dea.   The good goddess.

238. Nihil enim aliud potest rex, nisi id solum quod de jure potest.
For the king can only act according to law.

239. Rex debet esse sub lege, quia lex facit regem.
The king should be subject to the law, because the law makes the king.

239. In omnibus imperatoris excipitur fortuna; cui ipsas leges Deus subjecit.
The interest of the emperor is in all things to be reserved; to whom God has made the laws themselves subject.

239. Decet tamen principem servare leges, quibus ipse solutus est.
Nevertheless it becomes a prince to protect those laws from which he is himself exempt.

239. Præ.   Before.

239. Rogo.   To ask.

241. Majora et minora regalia.   The greater and lesser regalia.

241. Majora regalia imperii preeminentiam spectant; minora vero ad commodum pecuniarum immediate attinet; et hæc proprie fiscalia sunt, et ad jus fisci pertinent.
The greater royalties of the kingdom appertain to dignity of station: but the inferior immediately concern the acquisition of money; these are properly fiscal, and relate to the rights of the king's revenue.

241. Rex est vicarius et minister Dei in terra: omnes quidem sub eo sunt, et ipse sub nullo nisi tantum sub Deo.
The King is the vicegerent and minister of God on earth: all are subject to him; and he is subject to none but to God alone.

242. Ipse autem rex non debet esse sub homine, sed sub Deo, et sub lege, quia lex facit regem. Attribuat igitur rex legi, quod lex attribuat ei, videlicet dominationem, et potestatem; non est enim rex, ubi dominatur voluntas et non lex.

The king himself should not be subject to man but to God and the law, for the law makes the king. Therefore, the king should give to the law what the law gives to him, namely, dominion and power; for there can be no king where will, and not law, governs.

---

242. Basileus.	King.

---

242. Imperator.	Emperor.

---

242. Rex allegavit, quod ipse omnes libertates haberet in regno suo, quas imperator vindicabat in imperio.

The king alleged that he should possess the same privileges in his kingdom as an emperor claimed in his empire.

---

246. Nihil enim aliud, &c. [Vide ante, p. 238.]

---

247. Nullum tempus occurrit regi.	No time runs against the king.

---

247. Sunt etiam aliæ res quæ pertinent ad coronam, quæ non sunt ita sacræ, quem, transferri possunt, sicut sunt fundi, terra et tenementa; et hujusmodi per quos corona regis roborata et in quibus currit tempus contra regem, sicut contra quemlibet privatam personam.

There are also other things belonging to the crown that are not so sacred, and may be transferred, such as crown manors, lands and tenements, and things of this kind, by which the king's crown is strengthened, and in which time runs against the king, as against any private person.

---

248. Ipso facto.	By the fact itself.

---

249. Eo instanti.	From that moment—immediately.

---

249. Demissio regis vel coronæ.	The demise of the king or the crown.

---

250. In ejus unius persona veteris reipublicæ vis atque majestas per cumulatas magistratuum potestates exprimebatur.

All the power and majesty of the old commonwealth were concentrated in the person of that one man by the united powers of the magistrates.

---

254. Securitas legatorum, &c. [translated in the text.]

---

254. Comites.	Attendants.

---

254. Jure gentium.	By the law of nations.

254. Et quanquam visi sunt comisisse, ut hostium loco essent, jus tamen gentium valuit.

And although they were seen to have acted as enemies, nevertheless the law of nations prevailed.

254. Qui Romam fide publica venerat.

Who had come to Rome on the public faith.

254. Fit reus magis ex æquo bonoque quam ex jure gentium.

He was amenable rather on the score of natural equity, than by the law of nations.

256. Sæpe quæsitum est an comitum numero et jure habendi sunt, qui legatum comitantur, non ut instructior fiat legatio, sed unice ut lucro suo consulant, institores forte et mercatores. Et quamvis hos sæpe defenderint et comitum loco habere voluerint legati, apparet tamen satis eo non pertinere, qui in legati legationisve officio non sunt. Quum autem ea res nonnunquam turbas dederit, optimo exemplo in quibusdam aulis olim receptum fuit, ut legatus teneretur exhibere nomenclaturam comitum suorum.

It was often a question whether they who accompanied the embassador, not that the embassy might be better appointed, but merely to consult their own advantage, perhaps as hucksters and merchants, should be reckoned in the number and enjoy the rights of his train. And although the embassadors often protected them, and wished to reckon them in the number of their suite, yet it is evident that they who are neither in the office of embassador, nor employed in the embassy, do not belong to it. But as this frequently caused disturbances, it was formerly adjudged in some courts the best mode of proceeding, that the embassador should be bound to show a list of the names of his attendants.

257. Quoad hoc.   As to this.

257. Hostes hi sunt, qui nobis, aut quibus nos, publice bellum decrevimus: cæteri latrones aut prædones sunt.

Those are enemies who have publicly declared war against us, or against whom we have publicly declared war; all others are thieves or robbers.

259. Droits.   Rights.

260. Quam legem exteri nobis posuere, eandem illis ponemus.

We will impose the same law on foreign merchants that they have imposed on us.

261. Nobiliores natalibus, et honorum luce conspicuos, et patrimonio ditiores, perniciosum urbibus mercimonium exercere prohibemus.

We forbid those who are noble by birth, conspicuous from the splendor of their honors, and wealthy in their patrimony, to exercise traffic, so pernicious to cities.

261. Homo mercator vix aut nunquam potest Deo placere; et ideo nullus Christianus debet esse mercator; aut si voluerit esse projiciatur de ecclesia Dei.

A trader can seldom or never please God; therefore, no Christian ought to be a trader; or, if he will be one, he should be cast out from the church of God.

261. Falsa fit pœnitentia [laici] cum penitus ab officio curiali vel negotiali non recedit, quæ sine peccatis agi ulla ratione non prævalet.

The repentance [of a layman] becomes fallacious if he quit not entirely the professions of law and traffic, which it is impossible to exercise in any manner without sin.

263. Trinoda necessitas: scilicet pontis reparatio, arcis constructio, et expeditio contra hostem.

The threefold obligation: that is, to repair bridges, to build towers, and to serve against the enemy.

263. Erant in Anglia, quodammodo, tot reges vel potius tyranni, quot domini castellorum.

There were in England, in effect, as many kings, or rather tyrants, as there were lords of castles.

264. Regalia.   Royalties.

266. Ad hoc autem creatus est et electus, ut justitiam faciat universis.

But he is created and chosen for the purpose of dispensing justice to all.

267. Durante bene placito.   During pleasure.

267. Quamdiu bene se gesserint.
So long as they shall have conducted themselves uprightly.

268. Dicebatur fregisse juramentum regis juratum.
He was said to have broken the sworn oath of the king.

268. Sacramentum domini regis fregisse.
To have broken the oath of the king.

268. Non vult prosequi.   He will not prosecute.

273. Disputare de principali judicio non oportet; sacrilegii enim instar est, dubitare an is dignus sit quem elegerit imperator.

It is not fit to dispute concerning the judgment of the prince; for it is a kind of sacrilege to doubt the eligibility of him whom the emperor shall have chosen.

275. Compositio ulnarum et perticarum. Composition of yards and perches.

---

275. Compositio mensurarum.　　The composition of measures.

---

276. Pondus regis.　　The king's weight.

---

276. Mensura domini regis.　　The king's measure.

---

278. A Germanis enim, quos Angli Esterlingi ab orientali situ vocarunt, facta est appellatio, quos Johannes Rex ad argentum in suam puritatem redigendum primus evocavit, et ejusmodi nummis Esterlingi in antiquis scriptis semper concipiuntur.

For the appellation is derived from the Germans, called by the English Esterlings from their easterly situation, whom King John first sent for, to reduce silver to its pure state, and in ancient writings accounts are always reckoned in sterling money.

---

278. Religio reformata, pax fundata, moneta ad suum valorem reducta, &c.

Religion reformed, peace established, money restored to its due value, &c.

---

285. Valor beneficiorum.　　The value of benefices.

---

286. Terræ dominicales regis.　　The king' demesne lands.

---

287. Fundi patrimoniales.　　Lands of inheritance.

---

290. De prerogativo regis.　　Of the king's prerogative.

291. Omnes res suas liberas et quietas haberet.
That he should retain his property free and undisputed.

---

291. Quod enim jus habet fiscus in aliena calamitate ut re tam luctuosa compendium sectetur?
For what right has the exchequer in other men's misfortunes, that it should seek gain from so lamentable a source?

---

292. Quæ enim res in tempestate levandæ navis causa ejiciuntur, hæ dominorum permanent. Quia palam est, eas non eo animo ejeci, quod quis habere noluit.
Those things which are cast overboard for the sake of lightening the ship still belong to the owners. For it is clear that they were not thrown away as relinquished on any other account.

---

293. In naufragorum miseria et calamitate tanquam vultures ad prædam currere.
To run like vultures to their prey, amidst the misery and calamity of shipwrecked sufferers.

295. Vetus depositio pecuniæ.   The previous concealment of the money.

---

296. Jus commune et quasi gentium.
The common law, and as it were the law of nations.

---

296. Bona vacantia.   Goods having no claimant.

---

297. Ultimus hæres.   The last heir.

---

298. Primum coram comitibus et viatoribus obviis, deinde in proxima villa vel pago, postremo coram ecclesia vel judicio.

First before the inhabitants of the place and passing travellers, then in the next town or village, lastly before the church, or judgment-court.

---

298. Pecus vagans, quod nullus petit, sequitur, vel advocat.
Wandering cattle, which no one seeks, follows, or calls to.

---

299. Hæc quæ nullius in bonis sunt, et olim fuerunt inventoris de jure naturali jam efficiuntur principis de jure gentium.

Those things which are no man's property and formerly belonged to the finder as by natural right, become now the property of the king by the law of nations.

---

299. Bona confiscata.   Confiscated goods.

---

299. Expressio unius est exclusio alterius.
The expression of one thing is the exclusion of another.

---

299. Item de his quæ pro wayvio habentur, sicut de averiis, ubi non apparet dominus, et quæ olim fuerunt inventoris de jure naturali jam efficiuntur principis de jure gentium.

Also concerning those things which are accounted waifs, as of beasts of the plough, where the owner does not appear, and which were formerly the property of the finder by natural right, belong now to the king by the law of nations.

---

299. Averia.   Beasts of the plough

---

299. Omnia.   All things.

---

299. Quæ.   Things which.

---

300. Census regalis.   The royal revenue.

---

301. Omnia quæ movent ad mortem sunt Deo danda.
          What moves to death we understand
          Is forfeit as a deodand.
                    COWELL, Tit. Deodand.

301. Si quis, me nesciente, quocunque meo telo vel instrumento in perniciem suam abutatur; vel ex ædibus meis cadat, vel incidat in puteum meum, quantumvis tectum vel munitum, vel in cataractum, et sub molendino meo confringatur, ipse aliqua mulcta plectar; ut in parte infelicitatis meæ numeratur habuisse vel ædificasse aliquod quo homo periret.

If any one, without my knowledge, use any weapon or instrument of mine for his own destruction; or fall from my house, or into my well, however securely covered or fenced, or into my mill-stream, or be crushed in my mill, let me suffer by some fine; as the misfortune may be reckoned in part mine, to have built or possessed any thing by which a man should perish.

303. De idiota inquirendo.	Of inquiring concerning an idiot.
303. Purus idiota.	An absolute idiot.
303. A nativitate.	From his birth.
303. Non compos mentis.	Not in his right mind.
304. Idiota a casu et infirmitate.	An idiot by accident and infirmity.

305. Solent prætores, si talem hominem invenerint, qui neque tempus neque finem expensarum habet, sed bona sua dilacerando et dissipando profundit, curatorem ei dare, exemplo furiosi: et tamdiu erunt ambo in curatione, quamdiu vel furiosus sanitatem, vel ille bonos mores, receperit.

The prætors are accustomed, when they find a man who sets no bounds to his expenses, but lavishes his fortune in acts of dissipation, to appoint him a guardian as though he were a madman; and as the madman so the spendthrift shall be in wardship until the one be restored unto a sanity of mind and the other to reformed manners.

306. Sic utere tuo ut alienum non lædas.
Use your property in such a manner that you injure not that of another.

307. Quota.	Portion.
307. Quantum.	Quantity.
312. Verbatim.	Word for word.
314. Quædam nova consuetudo.	A certain new custom.

314. Ad emendum et vendendum sine omnibus malis tolnetis, per antiquas et rectas consuetudines.
For buying and selling free from all unjust tolls, according to ancient and proper customs.

314. Pro bono publico.	For the public good.
314. Custuma.	Customs.
314. Consuetudines.	Customs.
314. Costuma antiqua sive magna.	Ancient or great customs.
314. Costuma parva et nova.	New and small customs.
315. Ad valorem.	According to the value.
316. Quantum.	The amount.

316. Scavage.

A toll required of foreign merchants for goods offered for sale prohibited by the statute.

317. Remissum magis specie quam vi, quia cum venditor pendere juberetur, in partem pretii emptoribus accrescebat.

Remitted rather in appearance than reality, for when the seller was ordered to pay it, he enhanced proportionally the price to the buyers.

327. Pro tempore, pro spe, pro commodo, minuitur eorum pretium atque augescit.

Their price was lessened and increased according to time, expectation, or advantage.

339. Custodiam comitatus.	The custody of the county.
340. Incolæ territorii.	The inhabitants of the territory.
340. Ex quibus rex unum confirmabat.	Of whom the king confirmed one.
341. In crastino animarum.	On the morrow of All Souls.
341. Jura regalia.	Regal rights.

342. Non obstante aliquo statuto in contrarium.

Notwithstanding any statute to the contrary.

346. Eligebantur olim ad hoc officium potentissimi sæpenumero totius regni proceres, barones, comites, duces, interdum et regum filii.

Formerly the most powerful nobles, as barons, counts, dukes, and sometimes even the sons of kings, were frequently chosen for this office.

347. De coronatore eligendo.	Of choosing a coroner.

347. Quod talem eligi faciat, qui melius et sciat et velit et possit, officio illi intendere.

That he cause such one to be chosen as is the best informed, and most willing and able to hold that office.

347. Statutum de militibus.	The statute concerning soldiers.
348. De coronatore exonerando.	Of discharging the coroner.
348 De officio coronatoris.	Of the office of coroner.
348. Super visum corporis.	On the view of the body.
348. Oyer and terminer	To hear and determine.

348. De corpore delicti constare oportebat; i. e. non tam fuisse aliquem in territorio isto mortuum inventum quam vulneratum et cæsum. Potest enim homo etiam ex alia causa subito mori

It was necessary that the crime should be evident; that is, not merely that a person was found dead in that district, but that he was wounded and slain. For a man may die suddenly from other causes.

349. Custodes.	Keepers.
349. Conservatores pacis.	Keepers of the peace.

350. De probioribus et potentioribus comitatus sui in custodes pacis.
From the most upright and powerful of their county as keepers of the peace.

351. Ipsius patris beneplacito.	By the good pleasure of his father.

351. Quorum aliquem vestrum A, B, C, D, &c. unum esse volumus.
Of whom we will that some one of you, A, B, C, D, &c. be one.

352. Dedimus potestatem.	We have empowered.
352. Dedimus.	We have given.
353. Procedendo.	Proceeding.
354. Noli prosequi.	Do not prosecute.
355. Comes stabuli.	Count of the stable.
355. Pro hac vice.	For the occasion, or occasionally.

355. Plenam potestatem et auctoritatem damus et committimus ad cognoscendum et procedendum in omnibus et singulis causis et negotiis de et super crimine læsæ majestatis, seu, ipsius occasione, cæterisque causis qui-

buscunque, summarie et de plano, sine strepitu et figura judicii, sola facti
veritate inspecta.

We give and entrust to you full power and authority for taking cognizance of and proceeding in all and every cause and matter of and concerning
the crime of high treason, or, when occasion be, in every other cause, sum-
marily and clearly, without the noise and show of trial, the truth of the
fact alone being inquired into.

356. Excubias et explorationes quas wactas vocant.
Watches and searches which they call WACTAS.

357. Trinoda necessitas.   The threefold obligation.

357. Expeditio contra hostem, arcium constructio, et pontium reparatio.
Going against the enemy, construction of towers and reparation of
bridges.

357. Ad instructiones reparationesque itinerum et pontium, nullum genus
hominum, nulliusque dignitatis ac venerationis meritis, cessare oportet.
With respect to the construction and repairing of ways and bridges
no class of men of whatever rank or dignity should be exempted.

358. Curatores viarum.   Keepers of the ways.

362. Paterfamilias.   The father of a family.

363. Prima facie.   On the first view.

370. Nemo potest exuere patriam.   No one can renounce his country.

371. Ex vi termini.   From the sense of the expression.

371. Vita et membra sunt in potestate legis.
Life and limbs are in the power of the law.

372. Droit d'aubaine.
The right of inheriting the estate which an alien has at his death.

372. Jus albinatus.   Alien law.

373. Postliminium.
A return of one who had gone to sojourn elsewhere, or had been
taken by the enemy, to his own country, right, and estate, again.—A
recovery.

374. Coelum nec solum.   Neither the climate nor the soil.

374. Ex donatione regis.   By the gift of the king.

375. Ipso facto.   By that deed or circumstance.

377. Eundo, redeundo, et morando.   In going, returning, and remaining.

377. Per clerum et populum.   By the clergy and people.

378. "Nulla electio prælatorum (sunt verba Ingulphi) erat mere libera et canonica; sed omnes dignitates, tam episcoporum quam abbatum, per annulum et baculum regis curia pro sua complacentia conferebat." Penes clericos et monachos fuit electio, sed electum a rege postulabant.

"There was no election of prelates (says Ingulphus) purely free and canonical; but the king's court granted all dignities at its pleasure, as well of bishops as abbots, by the ring and the staff." The election was in the power of the clergy and monks, but they requested election by the king.

378. Per annulum et baculum.   By the ring and staff.

379. Per sceptrum.   By the sceptre.

379. Conge d'eslire.   Permission to elect.

380. Nolo episcopari.   I will not be made a bishop.

380. Et in episcopum Oxoniensem consecratus est anno 1455 nondum annos natus viginti. Anno deinde 1460 (id quod jure mirere) summus Angliæ factus est Cancellarius.

And he was consecrated Bishop of Oxford in the year 1455, not having yet attained the age of twenty. And (what is very surprising), in the year 1460 he was made High Chancellor of England.

380. Hoc sedente episcopus Sancti Andreæ in Scotia archiepiscopus per Sixtum Quartum creatus est; jussis illi duodecim episcopis illius gentis subesse, qui hactenus archiepiscopo Eboracensi suffraganei censebantur. Reclamante quidem Eboracensi, sed frustra; asserente pontifice, minime convenire, ut ille Scotiæ sit metropolitanus, qui, propter crebra inter Scotos ac Anglos bella, Scotis plerumque hostis sit capitalis.

In this assembly the Bishop of St. Andrew, in Scotland, was created archbishop by Sextus the Fourth; the twelve bishops of that nation, who were hitherto considered suffragans of the Archbishop of York, being commanded to be subordinate to him. Against this the Archbishop of York appealed, but in vain; the Pope asserting that it was in no wise fit that he should be the metropolitan of Scotland, who, on account of the frequent wars between the Scotch and English, was generally their chief enemy.

381. Primæ, or primariæ preces.   First prayers, or suits.

381. Rex, &c. salutem. Scribatis episcopo Karl. quod — Roberto de Icard pensionem suam, quam ad preces regis prædicto Roberto concessit, de cætero

solvat: et de proxima ecclesia vacatura de collatione prædicti episcopi, quam ipse Robertus acceptaverit, respiciat.

The king, &c. sends greeting. That you write to the Bishop of Carlisle, that he henceforth pay to Robert de Icard, the pension which he granted to the said Robert at the desire of the king: and that the aforesaid Bishop see that the said Robert be appointed to the next church vacancy in his collation.

384. Vicem seu personam ecclesiæ gerere. To represent the church.

387. Qui illi de temporalibus, episcopo de spiritualibus, debeat respondere.

Who should answer to him concerning temporal, to the bishop concerning spiritual, affairs.

387. Secundum regulas.	According to the rules.
389. Malum in se.	Crime in itself.
389. Schismaticus inveteratus.	An inveterate schismatic.
389. Malum prohibitum.	Fault because forbidden.
390. Minus sufficiens in literatura.	Deficient in learning.
390. Vicarius non habet vicarium.	A vicar has no deputy.
392. In utroque jure.	In both laws.
392. Juris utriusque doctor.	Doctor of both laws.

392. Ut nulla legatur palam et publice lectio in jure canonico sive pontificio, nec aliquis cujuscunque conditionis homo gradum aliquem in studio illius juris pontificii suscipiat, aut in eodem in posterum promoveatur quovis modo.

That no lecture be publicly read, in the canon or pontifical law, nor any man of whatsoever condition take any degree in the study of that law, or, henceforth be in any manner promoted in the same.

393. In commendam.	In trust.
393. Ecclesia commendata.	A living in trust.
393. Commendam retinere.	To retain a trust living.
393. Commendam recipere.	To receive a trust living.
393. De novo.	Anew.
393. Mandamus.	We command.

398. Quasi.   As.

398. Comites.   Earls.

398. A societate nomen sumpserunt, reges enim tales sibi associant.

They received their name from their society, because they were the king's companions.

399. In capite.   In chief, or of the king.

399. Faciemus summoneri archiepiscopos, episcopos, abbates, comites, et majores barones regni sigillatim per literas nostras, et præterea faciemus summoneri in generali per vicecomites et ballivos nostros omnes alios, qui in capite tenent de nobis ad certum diem, &c.

We will cause the archbishops, bishops, abbots, earls, and greater barons of the kingdom, to be severally summoned by our letters, and we will also cause all others, who hold of us in capite, to be summoned generally by our sheriffs and bailiffs for a certain day, &c.

401. Jure ecclesiæ.   By right of the church.

402. Pares.   Peers — equals.

402. In judicio non creditur nisi juratis.
No one is believed in court but upon his oath.

402. Scandalum magnatum.   Scandal of the peers.

403. Viri magnæ dignitatis.   Men of great dignity.

404. Domini.   Sirs.

404. Toga virilis.   The gown of manhood.

406. Jus imaginum.   The right of images.

406. Armigeri natalitii.   Esquires by birth.

406. Calcaribus argentatis.   With silver spurs.

406. Equites aurati.   Knights.

406. Certe altero hinc sæculo nominatissimus in patria jurisconsultus, ætate provectior, etiam munere gaudens publico et prædiis amplissimis, generosi titulo bene se habuit; forte, quod togatæ genti magis tunc conveniret civilis illa appellatio quam castrensis altera.

Certainly, in a former age, the most famous jurisconsult of his country, in advanced years, enjoying public reward, and ample estates, esteemed

himself happy in the title of GENEROSUS [equivalent to the word gentle-
man]; perhaps because this civic appellation suited the lawyer better
then, than the military title.

---

407. Probus et legalis homo.   A true and lawful man.

---

407. Quo warranto.   By what warrant.

---

407. Cæterum libertas et speciosa nomina prætexuntur; nec quisquam
alienum servitium et dominationem sibi concupivit, ut non eadem ista vo-
cabula usuparet.

But liberty and specious terms are made a pretext; nor has any one
ever desired a change of government who did not use those words.

---

408. De heretochiis.   Of heretochs or leaders.

---

408. Sapientes, fideles, et animosi.   Wise, faithful, and brave.

---

409. Prout eis visum fuerit, ad honorem coronæ et utilitatem regni.

As it should seem to them, for the honor of the crown and the advantage of the kingdom.

---

409. Isti vero viri eliguntur per commune consilium, pro communi
utilitate regni, per provincias et patrias universas, et per singulos comitatus
in pleno folkmote, sicut et vicecomites provinciarum et comitatuum, eligi
debent.

These men are chosen for the general benefit of the kingdom, by the
common council, by the provinces, the whole country, and by each county
in full assembly [folkmote], as also the sheriffs of provinces and counties
should be elected.

---

409. Reges ex nobilitate, duces ex virtute sumunt.

They chose their kings for their nobility, their leaders for their
valor.

---

409. Quum bellum civitas, aut illatum defendit aut infert, magistratus qui
ei bello præsint deliguntur.

When a city is engaged either in an offensive or defensive war,
magistrates qualified to direct that war are chosen.

---

410. Quod habeant et teneant, &c. [Vide post, vol. ii., p. 50.]

---

414. Nam neque quies gentium sine armis, neque arma sine stipendiis,
neque stipendia sine tributis, haberi queunt.

For neither can nations have peace without soldiers, soldiers without
pay, nor pay without taxes.

---

416. Misera est servitus ubi jus est vagum aut incognitum.

Wretched is the thraldom where the law is either uncertain or unknown.

---

417. Si milites quid in clypæo, &c. [translated in the text.]

---

423. Servi aut fiunt aut nascuntur: fiunt jure gentium, aut jure civili; nascuntur ex ancillis nostris.

Slaves are either born or made so; they are made slaves by the law of nations, or by the civil law; they are born slaves as the children of our female captives.

---

423. Mancipia, quasi manu capti.
Mancipia, as [manu capti] taken by hand.

---

423. Jure civili.   By the civil law.

---

424. Quid pro quo.   Value for value, or reciprocal compensation.

---

424. Jure naturæ.   By the law of nature.

---

425. Nolo episcopari.   I will not be made a bishop.

---

425. Intra mœnia.   Within the walls.

---

427. Pro tempore.   For a time.

---

429. Nam, qui facit per alium, facit per se.
For he who does a thing by the agency of another, does it himself.

---

429. Per quod servitium amisit.   By which he lost his service.

---

430. Nam, qui non prohibet cum prohibere possit, jubet.
For he who does not forbid a crime while he may, sanctions it.

---

431. Ob alterius culpam tenetur, sive servi, sive liberi.
Is held accountable for the fault of another, whether of his servant, or his child.

---

434. Consensus, non concubitus, facit nuptias.
Consent, not cohabitation, makes the marriage.

---

434. Pro salute animarum.   For the health of their souls.

---

434. Ab initio.   From the beginning.

---

435. Consanguinei.   Kindred.

---

435. Per verba de præsenti tempore.   By words of the present tense.

435. Ipsum matrimonium.   As marriage itself.

436. Duas uxores eodem tempore habere non licet.
It is not lawful to have two wives at one time.

436. Habiles ad matrimonium.   Fit for marriage.

438. Concubitu prohibere vago.   To forbid a promiscuous intercourse.

438. Quia non sua culpa, sed parentum, id commisisse cognoscitur.
Because she was considered to have committed it, not through her own fault, but that of her parents.

439. Per verba de futuro.   By words of the future tense.

439. In facie ecclesiæ.   In the face of the church.

439. Juris positivi.   Of positive law.

439. Juris naturalis aut divini.   Of natural or divine law.

440. A vinculo matrimonii.   From the bond of matrimony.

440. A mensa et thoro.   From bed and board.

441. Judex adulterii ante oculos habere debet et inquirere, an maritus pudice vivens, mulieri quoque bonos mores colendi autor fuerit. Periniquum enim videtur esse, ut pudicitiam vir ab uxore exigat, quam ipse non exhibeat.
A judge, in a case of adultery, should carefully examine, whether the husband by living chastely himself had also been an example of good conduct to his wife. For it seems perfectly unjust that the husband should require that chastity in his wife which appears not in himself.

441. De estoveriis habendis.   Of recovering estovers.

442. Nupta.   A wife.

442. A nubendo — tegendo.   From covering.

442. Post affidationem (id est futurarum nuptiarum conventio) et carnalem copulationem, sunt quasi.
After betrothing, (which is the agreement for the future marriage,) and carnal knowledge, they are, as it were, husband and wife.

442. Donatio mortis causa.
A donation to take effect in case of the death of the donor.

442. Nisi prius.   Unless before.

443. Dum sola.   Whilst unmarried.

443. Sui juris.   Capable of making a contract.

443. Nemo in propria causa testis esse debet.
No one should be a witness in his own cause.

443. Nemo tenetur seipsum accusare.   No one is bound to accuse himself.

444. Prochein amy.   Next friend—next of kin to an infant.

444. Aliter quam ad virum, ex causa regiminis et castigationis uxoris suæ, licite et rationabiliter pertinet.

Otherwise than lawfully and reasonably belongs to the husband for the due government and correction of his wife.

445. Flagellis et fustibus acriter verberare uxorem.
To beat his wife severely with scourges and sticks.

445. Modicam castigationem adhibere.   To use moderate chastisement.

446. Pater est quem nuptiæ demonstrant.
The nuptials show who is the father.

447. Judex de ea re cognoscet.
The judge shall take cognizance of that matter.

448. Tanquam testamentum inofficiosum.   As an unkind will.

449. Nudum pactum.   A barren compact.

449. In loco parentis.   In the place of a parent.

452. Patria potestas in pietate debet, non in atrocitate, consistere.
Paternal power should consist in kindness not in cruelty.

456. Enceinte.   Pregnant.

456. De ventre inspiciendo. For inspecting whether a woman be pregnant.

456. Rogaverunt omnes episcopi magnates, ut consentirent quod nati ante matrimonium essent legitimi, sicut illi qui nati sunt post matrimonium, quia ecclesia tales habet pro legitimis. Et omnes comites et barones una voce responderunt quod nolunt leges Angliæ mutare, quæ hucusque usitatæ sunt et approbatæ.

All the bishops requested the peers to consent that children born before marriage should be legitimate, as those which are born after marriage, because the church esteems them so. But all the earls and barons answered unanimously, that they would not change the laws of England which were hitherto used and approved.

457. Sit omnis vidua sine marito duodecim menses.
     Let every widow remain unmarried twelve months.

457. Infra annum luctus.   Within the year of mourning.

457. Extra quatuor maria.   Beyond the four seas.

457. Præsumitur pro legitimatione.
     The presumption is in favor of legitimacy.

459. Filius nullius.   The son of no one.

459. Contra.   Otherwise.

459. Filius populi.   The son of the people.

459. Casus omissus.   An omitted case.

460. Tutor.   A teacher.

460. Curator.   A guardian.

461. Nunquam custodia alicujus de jure alieni remanet, de quo habeatur suspicio, quod possit vel velit aliquod jus in ipsa hæreditate clamare.

     The guardianship of no person shall of right continue in him, of whom a suspicion may be entertained that he can or will claim any right in the inheritance.

461. Summa providentia.   The greatest prudence.

462.   —— pupillum O utinam, quem proximus hæres
     Impello, expungam.
     O were my pupil fairly knock'd o' th' head!
     I should possess th' estate if he were dead.
                     Dryden's Persius, s. ii., l. 23.

462. Quasi agnum committere lupo, ad devorandum.
     Like committing the lamb to the wolf to be devoured.

462. Ex parte paterna.   On the father's side.

462. Ex parte materna.   On the mother's side.

462. Pro tempore.   For a time.

464. Nisi convenissent in manum viri.

Unless they should come under the care of a husband.

464. Ad annum vigesimum primum; et eo usque juvenes sub tutelam reponunt.

To the twenty-first year; and they place their youths under guardianship till that period.

464. Prima facie.	On the first appearance.
464. Doli capax.	Capable of deceit.
465. Malitia supplet ætatem.	Malice is held equivalent to age.
465. Sub potestate parentis.	Under the power of a parent.
467. Ad studendum et orandum.	For study and prayer.
469. Universitates.	Universities.
469. Collegia.	Colleges.
469. Tres faciunt collegium.	Three make a college.
469. Si universitas ad unum redit.	If the university be reduced to one.

469. Et stet nomen universitatis.
And the name of "university" may remain.

470. Quatenus.	As.
471. Pro opere et labore.	For work and labor.
472. Illicitum collegium.	An unlawful college.

472. Neque societas, neque collegium, neque hujusmodi corpus passim omnibus habere conceditur; nam et legibus, et senatus consultis, et principalibus constitutionibus ea res coercetur.

Neither to all and everywhere is it allowed to have a society, college, or body of this kind; for the permission is controlled by the laws, by the decrees of the senate, and by the constitutions of the prince.

473. Creamus, erigimus, fundamus, incorporamus.
We create, we erect, we found, we incorporate.

474. Qui facit per alium, &c. [Vide ante, 429.]

476. Sodales legem quam volent, dum ne quid ex publica lege corrumpant, sibi ferunto.

Let the societies prescribe for themselves any law they please, provided it infringe not the public law.

---

477. Pro salute animæ.   For the health of the soul.

---

479. Gardianus et major pars sociorum.
The guardian and greater part of the society.

---

479. Magister.   The master.

---

479. Præpositus et major pars.   The governor and greater part.

---

479. Collegium, si nullo speciali privilegio subnixum sit, hæreditatem capere non posse, dubium non est.
There is no doubt that a college cannot take an inheritance unless by special privilege.

---

479. In mortua manu.   In a dead hand.

---

484. Sit visitator.   Let him be a visitor.

---

484. Visitationem commendamus. We recommend a visitation.

---

484. Si quid universitati debetur, singulis non debetur; nec quod debet universitas, singuli debent.
Whatever be due to an university, is not due to each member singly; nor is each singly answerable for the debts due from the university.

A

TRANSLATION,

&c., &c.

VOLUME THE SECOND.

3. ERANT omnia communia et indivisa omnibus, veluti unum cunctis patrimonium esset.

All things were common and undivided, as if there were but one patrimony for them all.

4. Quemadmodum theatrum, &c. [translated in the text.]

6. Colunt discreti et diversi; ut fons, ut campus, ut nemus placuit.

They dwelt separately, in different parts, as a fountain, plain, or grove pleased them.

8. Petitio principii.   Begging the question.

9. Publici juris.   Of public right.

11. Omni autem in re consensio omnium gentium lex naturæ putanda est.

But in everything the consent of all nations is to be considered as the law of nature.

11. Hæredes successoresque sui cuique liberi.

Every man's children are his heirs and successors.

18. Cujus est solum, ejus est usque ad cœlum.

Whoever has the land possesses all the space upwards to an indefinite extent.

19. Nomen generalissimum.   The most general name.

19. E converso.   On the other hand.

21. Jus patronatus.   The right of patronage.

23. Prava consuetudo.	An erroneous practice.
25. Jure divino.	By divine right.
28. Lex terræ.	The law of the land.
29. De modo decimandi.	Of a particular manner of tithing.
29. De non decimando.	Of an exemption from tithes.
29. Bona fide.	Actual — real — in good faith.
31. Felo de se.	A self-destroyer.

31. Ecclesia decimas non solvit ecclesiæ.
The church does not pay tithes to the church.

31. Arguendo.	In the course of argument.

31. Modus de non decimando non valet.
An exemption from tithing is of no force.

36. Sed secus.	But otherwise.
38. Charta de foresta.	Charter of the forest.
39. Campestres.	Those frequenting fields.
39. Sylvestres.	Those frequenting woods.
39. Aquatiles.	Water-fowls.
41. Assumpsit.	He undertook.
45. Pro tot. [totum]	Through the whole of the work.
45. Officina gentium.	The storehouse of nations.
45. Proprietas.	Property.
45. Totum.	The whole.

47. Sola, quæ de hostibus capta sunt limitaneis ducibus et militibus donavit; ita ut eorum ita essent, si hæredes illorum militarent, nec unquam ad privatos pertinerent: dicens attentius illos militaturos, si etiam sua rura defenderent. Addidit sane his et animalia et servos, ut possent colere quod acceperant; nec per inopiam hominum vel per senectutem deserentur rura vicina barbariæ, quod turpissimum ille ducebat.

The lands which were taken from the enemy on the borders he gave

to his generals and soldiers; on condition that their heirs should be
soldiers, and never belong to private stations: saying that they would fight
more resolutely, if they at the same time defended their own lands. He
also gave animals and slaves with them, that they might cultivate what
they had acquired; lest, through want of men, or by reason of old age, the
neighboring lands should be utterly neglected, a thing which he considered
most disgraceful.

47. Belluinas, atque ferinas, immanesque Longooardorum leges accepit.
     Received the wild, fierce and barbarous laws of the Lombards.

---

48. Jure belli.   By right of war.

49. Patriæ leges.   The laws of the country.

49. De more.   In the same manner.

49. Statuimus ut omnes liberi, &c. [Vide post, p. 50.]

49. Gulielmus rex, dux, &c.   William king, duke, &c.

49. Conquestor   Conqueror.

49. Beneficio concessionis cognati mei et gloriosi regis, Edwardi.
     By virtue of the grant of my cousin the glorious king Edward.

49. Ego Gulielmus, Dei dispositione et consanguinitatis hæreditate,
Anglorum basileus.
     I, William, king of England, by the dispensation of God and inheri-
tance of blood.

---

49. Rex tenuit magnum concilium, et graves sermones habuit cum suis
proceribus de hac terra; quo modo incoleretur, et a quibus hominibus.
     The king held a great council, and had important debates with his
nobles concerning this land, how it should be inhabited and by what men.

---

49. Omnes prædia tenentes quotquot essent notæ melioris per totam
Angliam ejus homines facti sunt, et omnes se illi subdidere, ejusque facti
sunt vasalli, ac ei fidelitatis juramenta præstiterunt, se contra alios quos-
cunque illi fidos futuros.
     All holding such estates as were of a better condition throughout
all England became his men, subjected themselves to him, were made
his vassals, and took the oath of fealty, that they would be faithful to
him against all, whomsoever they might be.

---

50. Statuimus, ut omnes liberi homines fœdere et sacramento affirment,
quod intra et extra universum regnum Angliæ Wilhelmo regi domino suo
fideles esse volunt; terras et honores illius omni fidelitate ubique servare
cum eo, et contra inimicos et alienigenas defendere.

We decree that all freemen bind themselves by homage and fealty, that within and without the whole kingdom of England, they will be faithful to King William their lord, and everywhere preserve his lands and honors with all fidelity, and defend him against all foreign and domestic enemies.

50. Omnes comites, et barones, et milites, et servientes, et universi liberi homines totius regni nostri prædicti, habeant et teneant se semper bene in armis et in equis, ut decet et oportet. et sint semper prompti et bene parati ad servitium suum integrum nobis explendum et peragendum, cum opus fuerit; secundum quod nobis debent de fœdis et tenementis suis de jure facere, et sicut illis statuimus per commune consilium totius regni nostri prædicti.

That all earls, barons, soldiers, servants, and freemen of our whole kingdom aforesaid, keep and hold themselves always well furnished with arms and horses, as is suitable and proper: and be always ready and well prepared for fulfilling and performing their entire service to us when need shall be; according to what they are by law bound to do for us by reason of their fees and tenements, and as we have ordained by the common council of our whole kingdom aforesaid.

51. Tout fuit in luy, et vient de luy al commencement.
All was his, and all proceeded originally from him.

53. Dedi et concessi.   I have given and granted.

54. Devenio vester homo.   I become your man.

55. Agri ab universis per vices occupantur: arva per annos mutant.
They all occupy the lands by turns: the arable lands they change annually.

55. Nec quisquam agri modum certum aut fines proprios habet; sed magistratus et principes, in annos singulos, gentibus et cognationibus hominum qui una coierunt, quantum eis et quo loco visum est, attribuunt agri, atque anno post alio transire cogunt.

Neither has any one a certain proportion or fixed boundaries to his land; but the magistrates and princes every year assign to the people, and the kindred of those men who have assembled together, as much land, and in whatever place, as seems to them fit, and oblige them the next year to remove from it to another portion.

56. Incertam et caducam hereditatem relevabat.
It raised up the uncertain and fallen inheritance.

56. In infinitum.   For ever.

59. Dominium directum.   Direct ownership.

61. Tenementum illud liberum, &c. [translated in the text.]

61.   Villenagiorum illud purum, &c. [translated in the text.]

63.   Auxilia fiunt de gratia et non de jure—cum dependeant ex gratia tenentium, et non ad voluntatem dominorum.

Aids arise from favor not from right—since they depend on the good will of the tenant, not on the will of the Lord.

64.   Erat autem hæc inter utrosque officiorum vicissitudo—ut clientes ad collocandas senatorum filias de suo conferrent; in æris alieni dissolutionem gratuitam pecuniam erogarent; et ab hostibus in bello captos redimerent.

But there was this reciprocity of service between them—that the clients should give a sum of money for marrying the daughters of their lords, pay their debts, and ransom them when taken captive in war.

64.   In capite.   In chief—or of the king.

64.   Confirmatio chartarum.   A confirmation of the charters.

66.   Hæres non redimet terram suam sicut faciebat tempore fratris mei, sed legitima et justa relevatione relevabo eam.

An heir shall not redeem his land as he used to do in the time of my brother, but I will release it for a just and lawful relief.

66.   Prima sæsina.   Primer seisin.

68.   Cessante causa, cessabit effectus.
The cause ceasing, the effect will cease also.

68.   Inquisitio post mortem.   An inquisition after death.

69.   In ipso consilio vel principum aliquis, vel pater, vel propinquus, scuto, frameaque juvenem ornant.   Hæc apud illos toga, hic primus juventæ honos: ante hoc domus pars videntur; mox reipublicæ.

In that council either some one of the princes, or the father, or relation, adorns the youth with a spear and buckler: this is the toga among them, the first honor of youth: before this ceremony, he was merely a member of his family, now, he becomes a member of the republic.

69.   De militibus.   Of soldiers.

70.   Duplex valor maritagii.   Double the value of the marriage.

71.   Hæredes maritentur absque disparagatione.
Heirs should be married without disparagement.

71.   Maritare.   To marry.

71.   Maritagium.   Marriage.

71. Ex vi termini.   From the strict sense of the word.

---

71. Sive sit masculus sive fœmina. Whether they be male or female.

---

74. Scutagium.   Scutage.

---

74. Servitium scuti.   Service money.

---

74. Nullum scutagium ponatur in regno nostro, nisi per commune consilium regni nostri.

Let no scutage be imposed but by the common council of our kingdom.

---

75. Pro feodo militari, &c. [translated in the text.]

---

77. In corde.   In the heart.

---

79. Id tenementum dici potest socagium.
That tenure may be called socage.

---

79. Illud dici poterit feodum militare.
That shall be called military tenure.

---

79. Ex donationibus, servitia militaria vel magnæ serjantiæ non continentibus, oritur nobis quoddam nomen generale, quod est socagium.

The general name of socage arises from grants to which military service, or grand sergeanty, is not incident.

---

81. Derivatio forte hæc nova et nostratibus adhuc inaudita, qui, a soc quatenus vel aratrum vel saltem vomerem signat, vocem derivare satagunt. Quam male tamen, eorum venia fusius a me jam monitum in tractatu de Gavelkind.

This derivation is perhaps new, and hitherto unheard of by our lawyers, who are very solicitous to derive the word from soc, as it signifies a plow or at least a ploughshare—but how erroneously, is, with their leave, shown more fully in my treatise on Gavelkind.

---

81. Dici poterit socagium a socco, et inde tenentes sockmanni, eo quod deputati sunt, ut videtur, tantummodo ad culturam, et quorum custodia et maritagia ad propinquiores parentes jure sanguinis pertinebant.

It may be called socage from soc, and hence, those holding under it sockmen, because they are only employed, as it seems, in the cultivation of the land, and whose wardship and marriage belong to their nearest relations by right of blood.

---

81. Socagium est servitium socæ. Socage is the service of the plough.

---

81. Feudum ignoble, plebeium, vulgare, Gall. FIEF ROTURIER, nobili opponitur, et proprie, dicimus, quod ignobilibus et rusticis competit, nullo feudali privilegio ornatum, nos socagium dicimus.

An ignoble, plebeian, vulgar fee, in French FIEF ROTURIER, as opposed to noble, and we may truly say, that it suits the ignoble and rustic, being adorned with no feudal privilege; we call it socage.

81.   Heretages en roture.   Plebeian inheritances.

81.   Manbote de villano et sokeman xii oras, de liberis autem hominibus iii marcas.
The compensation for the death of a villein, or sokeman, was xii ores, but for a freeman iii marks.

81.   Milites.   Soldiers.

81.   Sokemanni.   Sockmen.

82.   Liberum et commune socagium.   Free and common socage.

84.   Pater cunctos filios adultos a se pellebat, praeter unum quem haeredem sui juris relinquebat.
The father used to send away all his sons when grown up, excepting one who became his heir.

84.   In toto regno, ante ducis adventum, frequens et usitata fuit: postea caeteris adempta, sed privatis quorundam locorum consuetudinibus alibi postea regerminans: Cantianis solum integra et inviolata remansit.
It was general and customary through the whole kingdom before the arrival of the Duke; afterwards this tenure was abolished with the rest, reviving only in the private customs of certain places: with the Kentish men alone it remained inviolate and entire.

85.   In capite.   In chief—or of the king.

86.   Eo maxime praestandum est, ne dubium reddatur jus domini et vetustate temporis obscuretur.
It is chiefly to be taken, lest the right of the lord should be rendered doubtful and obscured by length of time.

87.   Quaedam praestatio loco relevii in recognitionem domini.
A certain praestation [sum of money paid] instead of a relief as an acknowledgment of the lord.

88.   Valor maritagii.   The value of the marriage.

90.   A manendo.   From remaining.

90.   Dominus manerii.   The lord of the manor.

91.   In infinitum.   Without limit.

91. Quia emptores.   Because purchasers.

91. Prerogativa regis.   The king's prerogative.

92. Vilis.   Vile.

92. A villa.   From a village.

93. Ille qui tenet in villenagio faciet quicquid ei præceptum fuerit, nec scire debet sero quid facere debet in crastino, et semper tenebitur ad incerta.

He who holds in villenage shall do whatsoever he is commanded, nor ought he to know on the evening of one day what he must do on the morrow, but shall always be held to an uncertain service.

93. Nullus liber homo capiatur vel imprisonetur.
No free man may be taken or imprisoned.

94. Partus sequitur ventrem.
The offspring follows the condition of its mother.

94. Nullius filius.   The son of nobody.

98. Indebitatus assumpsit.   Being indebted, he undertook.

99. Villana faciunt servitia, sed certa et determinata.
They perform villein services but certain and fixed.

99. Villanum soccagium.   Villein socage.

100. It ideo dicuntur liberi.   And therefore they are called free.

102. Omnium rerum immunitatem.   Exemption from all offices.

105. Absolutum et directum dominium.
The absolute and direct ownership.

105. Prædium domini regis est directum dominium, cujus nullus est author nisi Deus.
The estate of the king is direct ownership, of which God alone is the author.

106. Feodum est quod quis tenet sibi et hæredibus suis, sive sit tenementum, sive reditus, &c.
A fee is that estate which a man holds to himself and his heirs, whether it be a tenement or a rent.

106. Servitus est jus, quo res mea alterius rei vel personæ servit.
Service is that right by which my estate is answerable to the estate or person of another.

107. In esse.   In being.

107. Nam nemo est hæres viventis. For no one is the heir of the living.

107. In nubibus.   In the clouds.

107. In gremio legis.   In the bosom of the law.

108. Donationes sint stricti juris, ne quis plus donasse præsumatur quam in donatione expresserit.

Donations should be construed strictly, lest any one be presumed to have given more than is expressed in the donation.

108. Stricti juris.   Of strict right.

110. Donatio stricta et coarctata; sicut certis hæredibus, quibusdam a successione exclusis.

A strict and limited donation; as to certain heirs, others being excluded from the succession.

110. De donis.   Of gifts.

110. Si quis terram hæreditariam habeat, eam non vendat a cognatis hæredibus suis, si illi viro prohibitum sit, qui eam ab initio acquisivit, ut ita facere nequeat.

He who possesses an hereditary estate may not, by sale, deprive his heirs by consanguinity of it, if he be prohibited from so doing by him who first acquired the land.

112. De donis conditionalibus.   Of conditional gifts.

113. Quasi.   As if.

113. Per formam doni.   By the form of the gift.

113. Eo nomine.   By that name.

114. E converso.   On the other hand.

117. Pia fraus.   Pious fraud.

120. Pur auter vie.   For the life of another.

122. Actus Dei nemini facit injuriam. The act of God injures no man.

123. A vinculo matrimonii.   From the bond of matrimony.

124. Durante viduitate.   During widowhood.

126. Tenes per legem Angliæ.   Tenant by the curtesy of England.

126. Pro tenentibus per legem Angliæ. For tenants by the curtesy of England.

127. Pares curtis.   Peers of the court.

127. Impotentia excusat legem.   Want of power excuses the law.

129. Triens, tertia.   The third part.

129. Dotalitium.   Dower.

130. Ubi nullum matrimonium, ibi nulla dos.
Where there is no marriage there is no dower due.

130. A mensa et thoro.   From bed and board.

130. Dotalitii et trientis ex bonis mobilibus viri.
Of her dower and thirds from the moveable goods of her husband.

130. Concessio mirabilis et inaudita.
A wonderful and unheard of assignment.

131. Si uxor possit dotem promereri, et virum sustinere.
If the wife be entitled to dower and be marriageable.

131. Quia junior non potest dotem promereri, et virum sustinere.
Because one younger cannot be entitled to dower or be marriageable.

132. In transitu.   Passing through his hands.

132. De la plus belle.   Of the handsomest.

132. Ad ostium ecclesiæ.   At the church door.

133. Ex assensu patris.   By assent of the father.

133. In facie ecclesiæ, et ad ostium ecclesiæ; non enim valent facta in lecto mortali, nec in camera, aut alibi ubi clandestina fuere conjugia.

In the face of the church, and at the church door; for those made on a death-bed, in a chamber or elsewhere, where the nuptials have been private, are not valid.

133. Si mortuo viro uxor ejus remanserit, et sine liberis fuerit, dotem suam habebit—si vero uxor cum liberis remanserit, dotem quidem habebit, dum corpus suum legitime servaverit.

If the wife survive her husband and there be no children she shall have her dower—but if there be children she shall have her dower only so long as she lives chastely.

134. Dos rationabilis.   A reasonable dower.

---

134. De questu suo — De terris acquisitis et acquirendis.

Of his lands already in possession, and which may be acquired hereafter.

---

134. Quod dotam eam de tali manerio cum pertinentiis, &c.

That I will endow her of such a manor with its appurtenances, &c.

---

134. Sacerdos interroget dotem mulieris; et, si terra ei in dotem detur, tunc dicatur psalmus iste, &c.

The priest shall ask what is the woman's dower; and if land be given to her for her dower, then let that psalm be read, &c.

---

134. Ubi quis uxorem suam dotaverit in generali, de omnibus terris et tenementis.

Where any one shall have endowed his wife generally, with all his lands and tenements.

---

134. Assignetur autem ei pro dote sua tertia pars totius terrae mariti sui quae sua fuit in vita sua, nisi de minori dotata fuerit ad ostium ecclesiae.

But the third part of all the lands of which her husband was possessed in his life-time shall be assigned to her for her dower, except she has been endowed with less at the church door.

---

138. Pro tanto.   To that amount.

---

138. Durante viduitate.   During widowhood.

---

138. Dotem non uxor marito, sed uxori maritus affert; intersunt parentes et propinqui, et munera probant.

The wife does not bring the portion to the husband, but the husband to the wife; the parents and relations are present and approve of the gifts.

---

138. Viri, quantas pecunias ab uxoribus dotis nomine acceperunt, tantas ex suis bonis, aestimatione facta, cum dotibus communicant. Hujus omnis pecuniae conjunctim ratio habetur, fructusque servantur. Uter eorum vita superavit, ad eum pars utriusque cum fructibus superiorum temporum pervenit.

Whatever portion a wife has brought to her husband, an estimate being made, he adds as much from his own goods. An account is taken of all this money jointly, and the produce laid by. The share of both, with all the profits that have accrued, falls to the survivor.

---

141. Quare impedit.   Why he hinders.

---

143. Id certum est, quod certum reddi potest.

That is certain which can be made certain.

146. Instar omnium.   Equal to all.

---

159. Pignoris appellatione eam proprie rem contineri dicimus, quæ simul etiam traditur creditori. At eam, quæ sine traditione nuda conventione tenetur, proprie ηγροτηεςæ appellatione contineri dicimus.

The appellation of PLEDGE is properly given to that security which is delivered immediately to the creditor. But that which is bound by a naked compact without delivery we properly call A MORTGAGE.

---

160. Si non sequatur ipsius vadii traditio, curia domini regis hujusmodi privatas conventiones tueri non solet.

If delivery of the pledge itself do not follow, the king's court is not accustomed to take cognizance of private agreements of this kind.

---

160. Cum in tali casu possit eadem res pluribus aliis creditoribus tum prius tum posterius invadiari.

Since in such a case the same thing might be pledged to many creditors as well before as afterwards.

---

160. Qui prior est tempore potior est jure.
He who is prior in time has the stronger right.

---

160. De mercatoribus.   Of merchants.

---

161. Ut liberum tenementum.   As a freehold.

---

161. Puisse porter bref de novele disseisine, auxi sicum de franktenement.
A writ of novel disseisin may likewise carry with it the freehold.

---

161. Nullum simile est idem.   Things similar are not the same.

---

166. In præsenti.   Immediately.

---

166. In futuro.   At a future period.

---

168. Eo instanti.   From the instant.

---

170. Nemo est hæres viventis.   No one is heir to the living.

---

172. Inops consilii.   Without counsel.

---

174. En ventre sa mere.   In the womb.

---

176. Accessorium non ducit, sed sequitur, suum principale.
The accessory does not precede but follows his principal.

---

181. E converso.   On the other hand.

---

182. Per my et per tout.   By half and by all.

182. Quilibet totum tenet et nihil tenet; scilicet, totum in communi, et nihil separatim per se.

Each holds the entirety and yet holds nothing; that is, the entirety in common, and nothing separately by itself.

182. Per tout, et non per my.   By all, and not by the half.

184. Jus accrescendi.   The right of survivorship.

184. Pars illa communis accrescit superstitibus, de persona in personam, usque ad ultimam superstitem.

That common share accumulates to the survivors from one person to another even to the last survivor.

184. Jus accrescendi inter mercatores pro beneficio commercii locum non habet.

The right of survivorship does not hold among merchants, for the benefit of commerce.

185. Nemo invitus compellitur ad communionem.

No one is compelled to a joint possession against his will.

185. Si non omnes qui rem communem habent, sed certi ex his, dividere desiderant; hoc judicium inter eos accipi potest.

If only some of those who hold a thing in common desire a partition, this judgment may be received between them.

186. Jus accrescendi præfertur ultimæ voluntati.

The right of survivorship is preferred to the last will.

186. Nihil de re accrescit ei, qui nihil in re quando jus accresceret habet.

No part of the estate accrues to him, who has nothing in the estate when the right accrues.

189. Cujus est divisio, ulterius est electio.

She who makes the division has the last choice.

190. Mittere in confusum cum sororibus, quantum pater aut frater ei dederit, quando ambulaverit ad maritum.

To bring into hotchpot with her sisters, when she shall marry, as much as her father or brother may have given her.

194. Damage feasant.   Doing damage.

199. Juris et seisinæ conjunctio.   A conjunction of the right and seisin.

205. Consanguineos.   Relations.

205. Propositus.

The person in a table of consanguinity from whom all the degrees are reckoned.

205. Ratio.	Proportion.
207. Abavus.	A great great grandfather.
207. Proavus.	A great grandfather.
207. Avus.	A grandfather.
207. Pater.	A father.
208. Designatio personæ.	A designation of the person.
209. Seisina facit stipitem.	Seisin makes the stock.
211. Juris positivi.	Of positive law.

211. Successionis feudi talis est natura, quod ascendentes non succedunt.

The nature of feudal succession is such that those in the ascending line do not inherit.

211. Hæreditas nunquam ascendit.	The inheritance never ascends.
212. Feudum antiquum.	An ancient fee.
212. Feudum maternum.	A maternal fee.
212. Feudum novum.	A new fee.
212. Ut antiquum.	As ancient.

212. Descendit itaque jus, quasi ponderosum quid cadens deorsum recta linea, et nunquam reascendit.

Therefore the right descends, like a heavy weight falling downwards in a straight line, and never reascends.

212. Qui doit inheriter al pere, doit inheriter al fitz.

He who is heir to the father is heir to the son.

213. Pater aut mater defuncti, filio non filiæ hæreditatem relinquent . . . . Qui defunctus non filios sed filias reliquerit, ad eas omnis hæreditas pertineat.

The father or mother at their death shall leave their inheritance to their son not to their daughter . . . . If a man at his death leave no sons, but only daughters, then the whole inheritance shall belong to them.

215. Feuda individua.	An impartible fee.

216. Progressum est ut ad filios deveniret, in quem scilicet dominus hoc vellet beneficium confirmare.

It was customary for it to descend to the sons, that is, to him on whom the lord wished to settle the estate.

217. In infinitum.	For ever.

221. Frater fratri, sine legitimo haerede defuncto, in beneficio quod eorum patris fuit succedat: sin autem unus e fratribus a domino feudum acceperit, eo defuncto sine legitimo haerede, frater ejus in feudum non succedit.

A brother may succeed to his brother dying without a lawful heir, in the estate which was their father's: but if one of the brothers shall have received the fee from his lord, and die without a lawful heir, his brother does not succeed.

221. Nomen haeredis, in prima investitura expressum, tantum ad descendentes ex corpore primi vasalli extenditur; et non ad collaterales, nisi ex corpore primi vasalli sive stipitis descendant.

The name of heir expressed in the first investiture extends only to the descendants of the body of the first vassal, and not to the collaterals unless they descend from the body of the first vassal or stock.

221. Sub modo.	In a particular way.
222. Ut feudum paternum.	As a paternal fee.
222. Ut feudum antiquum.	As an ancient fee.
222. Feudum avitum.	An ancestorial fee.
224. In feudis vere antiquis.	In fees really ancient.
224. Jure representationis.	By right of representation.

225. Haeredes successoresque sui cuique liberi et nullum testamentum: si liberi non sunt, proximus gradus in possessione, fratres, patrui, avunculi.

Every man's children are his heirs and successors if there be no will. If there be no children the next in degree shall be seised, as brothers, uncles on the father's side, uncles on the mother's side.

227. Possessio fratris facit sororem esse haeredem.
The seisin of the brother makes the sister heir.

227. In feudis antiquis.	In ancient fees.
229. In feudis novis.	In new fees.
229. Ut antiquis.	As ancient fees.
229. In feudis stricte novis.	In fees strictly new.

232. A patre.   From the father.

---

232. Frater fratri uterino non succedet in hæreditate paterna.
     A brother shall not succeed in the paternal inheritance to his brother by the mother's side.

---

236. Ex parte materna.   On the mother's side.

---

236. Sur grant et render.   On the grant and render.

---

236. Ex parte paterna.   On the father's side.

---

238. Arguendo.   In the course of argument.

---

238. Obiter.   Cursorily.

---

245. Feudum apertum.   An open fee.

---

245. Propter defectum sanguinis.   Through failure of issue.

---

245. Ultimus hæres.   The last heir.

---

245. Propter delictum tenentis.   Through the fault of the tenant.

---

246. Dominus capitalis feodi loco hæredis habetur, quoties per defectum vel delictum extinguitur sanguis tenentis.
     The chief lord of the fee is accounted heir whenever the blood of the tenant is extinct either by failure of issue or corruption.

---

247. Qui contra formam humani generis converso more procreantur, ut si mulier monstrosum vel prodigiosum enixa sit, inter liberos non computentur. Partus tamen, cui natura aliquantulum addiderit vel diminuerit, ut si sex vel tantum quatuor digitos habuerit, bene debet inter liberos connumerari; et si membra sint inutilia aut tortuosa, non tamen est partus monstrosus.
     Those who are born with a form not human are not considered children; as when a woman by a perversion of nature brings forth something monstrous or prodigious. Nevertheless the offspring to which nature has only added, or from which withheld something, as if it should have six or only four fingers, ought to be reckoned among children; and though its limbs be useless or distorted, yet it is not a monstrous birth.

---

247. Jus trium liberorum.   The right of three children.

---

247. Qui ex damnato coitu nascuntur, inter liberos non computantur.
     Those who are the offspring of an illicit connection are not reckoned as children.

---

248. Bastard eigne.
     An elder son, born before the marriage of his parents.

248. Mulier puisne — Filius mulieratus.
A legitimate son, whose elder brother is illegitimate.

248. Concubina.	A concubine.

248. Mulier.	A wife.

252. Dum bene se gesserit.	Whilst he shall have conducted himself well.

257. Inter alia.	Among other things.

257. Eo quod desiit esse miles, &c. [Vide ante, vol., i. p. 132.]	

257. Civiliter mortuus.	Dead in law.

258. Quod nullius est, id ratione naturali occupanti conceditur.
That which belongs to no one, is by natural reason granted to the occupant.

259. Hæreditas jacens.	The unoccupied inheritance.

259. Nullum tempus occurrit regi.	No time runs against the king.

260. Casus omissus.	An omitted case

262. Terra firma.	Firm land.

262. De minimis non curat lex.
The law takes not cognizance of small things.

264. Usu rem capere.	To take the thing by use.

269. Ecclesiæ de feudo domini regis non possunt in perpetuum dari, absque assensu et consensione ipsius.
Advowsons, of which the king has the fee, cannot be given in perpetuity without his consent and approval.

270. Non licet alicui de cætero dare terram suam alicui domui religiosæ, ita quod illam resumat tenendam de eadem domo; nec liceat alicui domui religiosæ terram alicujus sic accipere, quod tradat illam ei a quo ipsam recepit tenendam: si quis autem de cætero terram suam domui religiosæ sic dederit, ut super hoc convincatur, donum suum penitus cassetur, ut terra illa domino suo illius feodi incurratur.
It is not lawful for any one to give his land to a religious house for the purpose of taking it again to hold of that house; neither is it lawful for any religious house thus to receive land in order to restore it to its original owner to hold of that house: but if any one shall have so given his land, and can be convicted of the fact, his gift shall be utterly void, and the land escheat to the lord of the fee.

270 Non obstante.   Notwithstanding.

270. De religiosis.   Of religious persons.

271. Ad quod damnum.   At what loss.

278. Et quod non habet principium, non habet finem.
And that which has no beginning has no end.

281. De bonis asportatis.   For carrying away the goods.

282. Si vasallus feudum dissipaverit, aut insigni detrimento deterius fecerit, privabitur.
If a vassal shall have wasted the fee, or lessened its value by any notorious injury, he shall be deprived of it.

284. Feloniæ, per quas vasallus amitteret feudum.
Felonies, by which the vassal would lose his fee.

285. Nemo miles adimatur de possessione sui beneficii, nisi convicta culpa, quæ sit laudanda per judicium parium suorum.
No soldier shall be removed from the possession of his benefice, unless convicted of some offence, which must be declared by the judgment of his peers.

285. Arbitranda, definienda.   To be judged, to be declared.

288. Possessiones in jurisdictionalibus non aliter apprehendi posse, quam per attournances et avirances, ut loqui solent; cum vasallus, ejurato prioris domini obsequio et fide, novo se sacramento novo item domino acquirenti obstringebat; idque jussu auctoris.
Possessions with a right of jurisdiction can only be taken by attorning or professing to become tenant, as it is usually called; when the vassal resigning his former obedience and faith, bound himself by a fresh oath to the new lord, and that by the command of his ancient lord.

288. Emptiones vel acquisitiones suas det cui magis velit. Terram autem quam ei parentes dederunt non mittat extra cognationem suam.
He may give his purchases or acquisitions to whomsoever he pleases. But the land which descended to him he cannot alien from his kindred.

289. Si questum tantum habuerit is, qui partem terræ suæ donare voluerit, tunc quidem hoc ei licet: sed non totum questum, quia non potest filium suum hæredem exhæredare.
If he, who wishes to give a part of his land, has only what he has acquired himself, he may lawfully do it: but he cannot alien the whole, because he cannot disinherit his son and heir.

291. Sub modo.   In a certain degree.

291. Dum fuit non compos mentis suæ, ut dicit.
　　While he was of unsound mind, as he says.

291. Ore tenus.　　　　　　　　By word of mouth.

295. Κατ' εξοχην.　　　　　　　By way of pre-eminence.

295. Instar dentium.　　　　　　Like teeth.

298. Habendum et tenendum.　　To have and to hold.

299. Tenendum per servitium militare, in burgagio, in libero socagio.
　　To hold by military service, in burgage, in free socage.

299. De capitalibus dominis feodi.　Of the chief lords of the fee.

305. Propria manu pro ignorantia literarum signum sanctæ crucis expressi et subscripsi.
　　On account of my ignorance of letters, I have impressed and subscribed with my own hand the sign of the holy cross.

306. Normanni chirographorum, &c. [translated in the text.]

307. Unumquodque dissolvi potest eodem ligamine quo ligatum est.
　　Every thing may be annulled by the same means that made it.

307. Brevia testata.　　　　　　Short evidences.

307. Hiis testibus Johanne Moore, Jacobo Smith, et aliis. ad hanc rem convocatis.
　　Witness John Moore, Jacob Smith and others, for this purpose assembled.

307. Coram paribus.　　　　　　Before the peers.

307. Teste comitatu, hundredo, &c.　Witness the county, hundred, &c.

308. In cujus rei testimonium huic chartæ (vel scripto) nostra sigilla apposuimus. Iiis testibus, &c.
　　In witness whereof we have set our seals to this charter (or writing). Witness, &c.

308. Ab initio.　　　　　　　　From the beginning.

308. Ex post facto.　　　　　　After the fact.

310. Donatio feudi.　　　　　　The gift of a fee.

310. Tenor est qui legem dat feudo.

It is the condition or tenor of the deed which gives validity to a fee.

310. Modus legem dat donationi.   Measure gives validity to the grant.

310. Ne quis plus donasse, &c. [Vide ante, p. 108.]

311. Nam feudum sine investitura nullo modo constitui potuit.
For a fee can in no wise be perfected without investiture.

311. Fit juris et seisinæ conjunctio.
There is a conjunction of law and seisin.

312. Plenum dominium.   Absolute ownership.

312. Nam apiscimur possessionem corpore et animo; neque per se corpore, neque per se animo. Non autem ita accipiendum est, ut qui fundum possidere velit, omnes glebas circumambulet; sed sufficit quamlibet partem ejus fundi introire.

To obtain possession, we must enter on the land with an intention to possess, neither entry nor intention alone being sufficient. But it is not to be understood, that he who wishes to take possession must walk over every clod, for it is enough if he enter on any part of the land.

312. Traditionibus dominia rerum, non nudis pactis, transferuntur.
The ownership of a thing is transferred by delivery, not by mere agreement.

312. Jus ad rem.   A right to the thing.

312. Jus in re.   A right in the thing.

312. Non jus, sed seisina, facit stipitem.
Not right, but seisin, makes the stock.

314. Nam quod semel meum est, amplius meum esse non potest.
For what is once mine, cannot be mine more fully.

315. Pares debent interesse investituræ feudi, et non alii.
The peers, and no others, should be present at the investiture of the fee.

317. Traditio nihil aliud est quam rei corporalis de persona in personam, de manu in manum, translatio aut in possessionem inductio; sed res incorporales, quæ sunt ipsum jus rei vel corpori inhærens, traditionem non patiuntur.

Livery is merely the transferring from one person to another, from one hand to another, or the induction into possession of a corporeal hereditament; but an incorporeal hereditament, which is the right itself to a thing, or inherent in the person, does not admit of delivery.

318. In præsenti.   Immediately.

318. Jure uxoris.   In right of his wife.

321. Pro rata.   In proportion.

322. Communibus annis.   Upon an average.

327. Defaire, Infectum reddere.   To defeat.

327. Fidei-commissum.   A trust.

327. Usus fructus.   The usufruct.

328. Prætor fidei commissarius.   The judge of trusts.

330. Quæ ipso usu consumuntur.   Which are consumed by the use itself.

330. Æquitas sequitur legem.   Equity follows law.

338. Custos rotulorum.   Keeper of the Rolls.

340. Simplex obligatio.   A simple obligation.

340. Præmium pudoris.   The wages of shame.

340. Præmium pudicitiæ, or, concubinati.   The price of her chastity.

340. De novo.   Anew.

340. Turpis contractus.   An improper contract.

341. Solvit ad diem.   He paid it on the day.

341. Is cui cognoscitur.   He to whom it is acknowledged.

341. Is qui cognoscit.   He who acknowledges.

347. Ex speciali gratia, certa scientia, et mero motu regis.
     By the special favor, certain knowledge, and mere motion of the king.

348. Sur conusance de droit come ceo, &c.
     On the acknowledgment of the right, as that, &c.

348. Sur done, grant et render.   On the gift, grant, and surrender.

348. Sur conusance de droit tantum.
     On the acknowledgment of the right only.

348. Sur concessit.   On the grant.

349. Non in regno Angliæ providetur, vel est aliqua securitas major vel solennior, per quam aliquis statum certiorem habere possit, neque ad statum suum verificandum aliquid solennius testimonium producere, quam finem in curia domini regis levatum: qui quidem finis sic vocatur, eo quod finis et consummatio omnium placitorum esse debet, et hac de causa providebatur

There is no greater or more common security provided in the king-. dom of England, or by which a person can acquire a surer title, than by a fine levied in the king's court: nor can any testimony be produced more customary for confirming a title. It is called a fine because it is finis, that is, the end and consummation of all suits; and for this purpose it was provided.

349. Modus levandi fines.   The manner of levying fines.

349. Warrantia chartæ.   Warranty of the deed.

349. De consuetudinibus et servitiis.   Of customs and services.

350. Dedimus potestatem.   We have given power.

356. In statue quo.   As they were before.

357. Partes finis nihil habuerunt.
The parties to the fine had no interest in the land.

358. Præcipe quod reddat.   Command him to restore.

360. Astuti.   Cunning.

362. Ex provisione viri.   By the provision of her husband.

362. Actores fabulæ.   Actors of the fiction.

365. Coram non judice.   Before a judge not having jurisdiction.

367. Quando hasta vel aliud corporeum quidlibet porrigitur a domino se investituram facere dicente; quæ saltem coram duobus vasallis solemniter fieri debet.

When a spear, or other corporeal thing, is presented by the lord, saying, that he hereby invested him; which should be solemnly done in the presence of at least two vassals.

369. Mandamus.   We command.

375. In extremis.   In his last moments.

376. Quoad.   As to.

379. Pro tanto.   For so much.

---

379. Verba intentioni debent inservire.
Words should be subservient to the intention.

---

379. Benigne interpretamur chartas propter simplicitatem laicorum.
We interpret deeds favorably on account of the ignorance of the laity.

---

379. Quoties in verbis nulla est ambiguitas, ibi nulla expositio contra verba fienda est.
Where there is no ambiguity in the words, they should be construed according to their obvious meaning.

---

379. Nam qui hæret in litera, hæret in cortice.
For he who confines himself to the letter, goes but half way.

---

379. Mala grammatica non vitiat chartam.
Bad grammar does not vitiate a deed.

---

379. Nam ex antecedentibus et consequentibus fit optima interpretatio.
For a deed is best interpreted by the bearing of all its parts.

---

380. Nam verba debent intelligi cum effectu, ut res magis valeat quam pereat.
For words should be understood with an effect that may tend more to strengthen than destroy the subject matter.

---

386. Il conviendroit quil fust non mouuable et de duree a tousiours.
It must be immoveable and last forever.

---

386. Cateux sont meubles et immeubles: si comme vrais meubles sont qui transporter se peuvent, et ensuivir le corps; immeubles sont choses qui ne peuvent en suivir le corps, niestre transportees, et tout ce qui n'est point en heritage.
Chattels are moveable and immoveable: those which can be transported and follow the person are moveable; immoveable chattels are such as cannot follow the person, or be transported from place to place; and everything which is not in the inheritance.

---

390. Domitæ.   Of a tame nature.

---

390. Partus sequitur ventrem.
The offspring follows the condition of the mother.

---

390. Si equam meam equus tuus pregnantem fecerit, non est tuum sed meum quod natum est.
If my mare be with foal by your horse, the offspring is not yours but mine.

391. Cessante ratione cessat et ipsa lex.
The reason ceasing the law itself ceases.

391. Per industriam, propter impotentiam, propter privilegium.
By industry, by impotency in the animal, by privilege.

391. Mansueta, quasi manui assueta. Tame, as accustomed to the hand.

392. Animum revertendi.   The intention of returning.

392. Revertendi animum videntur desinere habere tunc, cum revertendi consuetudinem deseruerint.
They seem no longer to have the intention of returning when they forsake the custom.

393. Ratione soli.   On account of the soil.

394. Custos horrei regii.   The guard of the royal granary.

394. Si quis felem, horrei regii custodem, occiderit vel furto abstulerit, felis summa cauda suspendatur, capite aream attingente, et in eam grana tritici effundantur, usquedum summitas caudæ tritico co-operiatur.
If any one should kill or steal a cat, being the guard of the royal granary, the cat shall be suspended by the end of its tail, its head touching the floor, and they shall pour on it small measures of wheat until the tip of the tail be covered.

397. Rem in bonis nostris habere intelligimur, quotiens ad recuperandum eam actionem habeamus.
We are supposed to have a property in our goods whenever we can have an action to recover them.

397. Æque bonis adnumerabitur etiam, si quid est in actionibus, petitionibus, persecutionibus. Nam et hæc in bonis esse videntur.
All things to which we have a right by action, petition, or prosecution, are justly reckoned among our possessions. For these also appear to belong to us.

397. In potentia.   In possibility.

397. In esse.   In being.

402. Quare domum ipsius A. apud W. (in qua idem A. quendam H. Scotum per ipsum A. de guerra captum tanquam prisonem suum, quousque sibi de centum libris, per quas idem H. redemptionem suam cum præfato A. pro vita sua salvanda fecerat satisfactum foret, detinuit) fregit, et ipsum H. cepit et adduxit, vel quo voluit abire permisit, &c.
Wherefore he broke into the house of the said A. at W. (in which

the said A. detained a certain Scotchman named H., taken by him in battle, as his prisoner, until he should satisfy him in the sum of one hundred pounds, which he had agreed upon as his ransom with the aforesaid A. for saving his life) and took the said H. and carried him away, or permitted him to go wherever he pleased.

402. Spes recuperandi.   The hope of recovering it.

406. Si in chartis membranisve tuis carmen vel historiam vel orationem Titius scripserit, hujus corporis non Titius sed tu dominus esse videris.

If Titius shall have written any poem, history, or speech on your paper or parchment, the manuscript belongs to you, not to him.

407. Sui generis.   Of a particular kind.

411. Ferre igitur bestiæ, et volucres, et omnia animalia quæ mari, cœlo et terra nascuntur, simul atque ab aliquo capta fuerint, jure gentium statim illius esse incipiunt. Quod enim nullius est, id naturali ratione occupanti conceditur.

Therefore, wild beasts and birds, and all animals which are produced in air, sea, or earth, when taken by any one, immediately become his property by the law of nations. For that which belongs to no one, belongs by natural reason to the taker.

412. Qui alienum fundum ingreditur, venandi aut aucupandi gratia, potest a domino prohiberi ne ingrediatur.

He who enters on another man's ground for the purpose of hunting or fowling may be prohibited from so doing by the owner.

412. Venationes, et sylvaticas vagationes cum canibus et accipitribus.
Hunting and excursions in the woods with hawks and hounds.

413. In majorem cautelam, si qua forte sit irregularitas.
For greater caution, lest by chance there should be any irregularity.

414. Vita omnis in venationibus atque in studiis rei militaris consistit.
Their whole life consists in hunting, and the study of military affairs.

414. Quoties bella non ineunt, multum venatibus, plus per otium transigunt.
Whenever they are not engaged in war they pass much time in hunting, and still more in idleness.

415. Sit quilibet homo dignus venatione sua, in sylva, et in agris, sibi propriis, et in dominio suo: et abstineat omnis homo a venariis regiis, ubicunque pacem eis habere voluerit.

Let every man be entitled to hunt in his own wood, fields, and manor: and let every man abstain from the royal forests, if he wish to live in peace.

415. Cuique enim in proprio fundo quamlibet feram quoquo modo venari permissum.

For every one is permitted to hunt any wild animal on his own grounds, in whatever manner he pleases.

---

416. Capturam avium per totam Angliam interdixit.

He forbad fowling throughout all England.

---

419. Propter privilegium.   By privilege.

---

419. Bona vacantia.   Goods in which no man can claim a property.

---

419. Bona et catalla.   Goods and chattels.

---

419. Nullius in bonis.   The property of no one.

---

419. Quilibet homo dignus, &c. [Vide ante, p. 415.]

---

419. Quodam modo.   In a certain manner.

---

419. Quant beastes savages le roye aler hors del forrest, le property est hors del roy.

When the king's wild beasts get out of the forest he loses his property in them.

---

419. Silz sount hors del parke capienti conceditur.

If they be out of the park they become the property of the taker.

---

419. Ratione privilegii.   By reason of their privilege.

---

419. In æquali jure potior est conditio possidentis.

When there is equal right on both sides that of the possessor prevails.

---

424. Est quidem alia præstatio quæ nominatur heriettum; ubi tenens, liber vel servus, in morte sua, dominum suum, de quo tenuerit, respicit de meliori averio suo, vel de secundo meliori, secundum diversam locorum consuetudinem.

There is indeed another præstation, which is called a heriot; where a tenant at his death, whether a freeman or a slave, acknowledges the lord of whom he held, by giving his best beast or the second best, according to the custom of the place.

---

424. Magis fit de gratia quam de jure.

It is more a matter of favor than of right.

---

425. Si decedens plura habuerit animalia, optimo cui de jure fuerit debitum reservato, ecclesiæ suæ, sine dolo, fraude, seu contradictione qualibet, pro recompensatione subtractionis decimarum personalium, necnon et

oblationum, secundum melius animal reservetur, post obitum, pro salute animæ suæ.

If a man when dying shall have many animals, the best being reserved for him to whom it was of right due, let the second best, after his death, be set apart for the church for the good of his soul, without any deceit, fraud, or objection, as an amends for the withholding of personal tithes and oblations.

425. Symbolum animæ.   Passport of the soul.

426. Imprimis autem debet quilibet, qui testamentum fecerit, dominum suum de meliori re quam habuerit recognoscere; et postea ecclesiam de alia meliori.

Whosoever shall make a will, should in the first place acknowledge his lord by a bequest of the best chattel he may possess; and afterwards the church by the second best.

425. In quibusdam locis habet ecclesia melius animal de consuetudine: in quibusdam secundum, vel tertium melius; et in quibusdam nihil: et ideo consideranda est consuetudo loci.

In some places the church has the best animal by custom: in others the second or third best; and in others again nothing: and therefore it is the custom of the place which determines the matter.

428. Dignitatem istam nacta sunt, ut villis, sylvis, et ædibus, aliisque prædiis, comparentur; quod solidiora mobilia ipsis ædibus ex destinatione patrisfamilias cohærere videantur, et pro parte ipsarum ædium æstimentur.

Have obtained this estimation; that they are classed with towns, woods, houses, and other estates; because the more solid moveables seem to be fixed to the houses by the will of the ancestor, and are considered as a part of the buildings themselves.

429. De humatione unum tenendum est, contemnendam in nobis, non negligendam in nostris; ita tamen mortuorum corpora nihil sentire intelligamus—Quantum autem consuetudini famæque dandum sit, id curent vivi.

With respect to interment one rule is to be followed: we should be indifferent to it with respect to ourselves, but not neglect it with respect to our relatives; for notwithstanding we know the bodies of the dead to be insensible, yet whatever is due to custom, or reputation, should be the care of the living.

443. Ex contractu.   Arising from a contract.

443. Quasi ex contractu.   From something in the nature of a contract.

444. In omnibus contractibus, &c. [translated in the text.]

444. Do ut des.   I give, that you may give.

444. Facio ut facias.　　　　　I do, that you may do.

445. Facio ut des.　　　　　　I do, that you may give.

445. Do ut facias.　　　　　　I give, that you may do.

445. Servus facit ut herus det.　The servant performs, that the heir may give.

445. Herus dat ut servus faciat.
　　The heir gives, that the servant may perform.

445. Contra bonos mores.　　　Against good manners.

445. Neque verbis præscriptis solemnibus vestitum est, neque facto aut datione rei transiit in contractum innominatum.
　　Which is neither clothed in solemn and prescribed words, nor by any act or pledge has passed into an implied contract.

445. Ex nudo pacto non oritur actio.
　　An action cannot be founded on a barren or unconditional contract.

448. Emptionis-venditionis contractæ argumentum.
　　A token of a contract for purchase and sale.

448. Venditio per mutuam manuum complexionem.
　　A sale by the mutual joining of hands.

452. Jura enim nostra dolum præsumunt si una non pereant.
　　For our laws presume guile if they do not perish together.

453. Commodatum.　　　　　A lending.

453. Locatio.　　　　　　　A hiring.

457. Partem pro toto.　　　　A part for the whole.

458. Fœnus nauticum.　　　　Naval usury.

458. Usura maritima.　　　　Maritime usury.

458. Expressio unius est exclusio alterius.
　　The naming of one thing is the exception of another.

462.　　Romani pueri longis rationibus assem
　　　Discunt in partes centum diducere.　Dicat
　　　Filius Albini, si de quincunce remota est
　　　Uncia, quid superet? poterat dixisse, triens; eu
　　　Rem poteris servare tuam! redit uncia, quid fit?
　　　Semis.

But as for us, our Roman youths are bred
To trades, to cast accounts, to write and read:
Come hither, child, (suppose 'tis Albine's son)
Hold up thy head; take five from forty-one;
And what remains? Just thirty-six: Well done.
Add seven, what makes it then? Just forty-eight:
Ah, thou must be a man of an estate!

CREECH'S HORACE, p. 325., l. 487.

---

463. Qui tam.   Who as well.

---

469. Omissis omnibus aliis negotiis.   All other business being laid aside.

---

472. De debitore in partes secando. Of cutting the debtor into pieces.

---

472. Trans Tiberim.   Beyond the Tiber.

---

472. Mons sacer.   The sacred mount.

---

473. Omni quoque corporali cruciatu semoto.
All bodily torture being also removed.

---

473. Inhumanum erat spoliatum fortunis suis in solidum damnari.
It was inhuman, being deprived of all his fortune, to be utterly
ruined.

---

477. A vinculo matrimonii.   From the bond of matrimony.

---

480. Quantum indemnificatus. To what amount he should be indemnified.

---

483. Si quid misericordiæ causa ei fuerit relictum, puta menstruum vel
annum, alimentorum nomine, non oportet propter hoc bona ejus iterato
venundari: nec enim fraudandus est alimentis cottidianis.
If any thing shall have been left him through compassion, suppose
monthly or yearly, as a maintenance, he is not obliged on this account
again to sell his goods: for he is not to be deprived of his daily subsistence.

---

485. In auter droit.   In right of another.

---

487. In pari passu.   In an equal degree.

---

490. Ab intestato.   From an intestate.

---

491. Sive quis incuria, sive morte repentina, fuerit intestatus mortuus,
dominus tamen nullam rerum suarum partem (præter eam quæ jure debetur
hereoti nomine) sibi assumito. Verum possessiones uxori, liberis, et cog-
natione proximis, pro suo cuique jure, distribuantur.
If any one through negligence or sudden death die intestate, let not
the lord take any part of his effects, except what is due to him of right as

a heriot. But let his possessions be distributed among his wife, children, and next of kin, to every one according to their right.

---

492. De rationabili parte bonorum.
    Of the reasonable part, or share, of the goods.

---

492. Omnia catalla cedant defuncto; salvis uxori ipsius et pueris suis rationabilibus partis suis.
    Let them resign all the chattels to the will of the deceased; reserving to his wife and children their reasonable shares.

---

492. Quod cum per consuetudinem totius regni Angliæ hactenus usitatam et approbatam, uxores debent et solent a tempore, &c. habere suam rationabilem partem bonorum maritorum suorum: ita, videlicet, quod si nullos habuerint liberos, tunc medietatem: et si habuerint, tunc tertiam partem, &c.
    That as by the universal custom of England, hitherto used and approved, wives have a right and are accustomed from time, &c. to have a reasonable share of their husbands' goods, in the following proportion; that if they have no children, they shall take the half: and if they have children, then the third part, &c.

---

494. Parens patriæ.   Parent of the country.

---

494. In pios usus.   To pious uses.

---

495. Quod ordinarii, hujusmodi bona nomine ecclesiæ occupantes, nullam vel saltem indebitam faciunt distributionem.
    That the ordinaries, who take possession of goods of this kind in the name of the church, make no distribution of them, or at least no due distribution.

---

495. In Britannia tertia pars bonorum decedentium ab intestato in opus ecclesiæ et pauperum dispensanda est.
    In Britain a third part of the goods left by an intestate is to be distributed for the benefit of the church and the poor.

---

497. Non compotes.   Not in their right senses.

---

497 Animum testandi.   Testamentary discretion.

---

497. Liberum animum testandi.   Free will in making their testament.

---

498. In potestate parentis.   In the power of the parent.

---

498. Donatio mortis causa.
    A donation depending on the event of the death of the donor.

---

498. In auter droit.   In the right of another.

498. Jus disponendi. The right of disposal.

499. Quod libera sit cujuscunque ultima voluntas.
That the last will of every one be free.

499. Testatio mentis. A testifying of the mind.

499. Testari. To show or testify.

499. Juramentum. An oath.

499. Incrementum. An increase.

499. Voluntatis nostræ, &c. [translated in the text.]

502. In extremis. In his last moments.

502. Nam omne testamentum morte consummatum est, et voluntas testatoris est ambulatoria usque ad mortem.

For every testament is established by death, and the will of the testator is revocable until his death.

503. Querela inofficiosi testamenti. Complaint of an unkind will.

503. Cum testamento annexo. With the will annexed.

503. Durante minore ætate. During minority.

503. Durante absentia. During absence.

503. Pendente lite. Pending a suit.

504. Cum testamento annexo. With the will annexed.

504. Testamenti executores esse debent ii quos testator ad hoc elegerit, et quibus curam ipse commiserit; si vero testator nullos ad hoc nominaverit, possunt propinqui et consanguinei ipsius defuncti ad id faciendum se ingerere.

Those should be executors of a will whom the testator shall have chosen, and to whom he himself shall have committed the trust; but if the testator shall not have named any, the relations of the deceased may take this duty upon themselves.

504. Terminus a quo. The limit from which.

504. Jure mariti. Concerning the right of the husband.

505. Ad colligendum bona defuncti.
For collecting the goods of the deceased.

506. Ultimus hæres.   The last heir.

506. De bonis non.   Of the goods not administered.

506. Scire facias.   That you make known.

508. Pendent lite.   During a suit.

508. Per testes.   By witnesses.

509. Solidos legales.   Lawful shillings.

511. Servitia servientium et stipendia famulorum.
     The services of attendants and the wages of servants.

512. Scire facias.   That you make known.

512. Non ejusdem generis.   Not of the same kind.

512. In loco parentis.   In the place of a parent.

512. Inter se.   Among themselves.

512. De bonis defuncti primo deducenda sunt ea quæ sunt necessitatis, et
postea quæ sunt utilitatis, et ultimo quæ sunt voluntatis.
     From the effects of the deceased are to be answered, first, the de-
mands of necessity; afterwards, what expediency requires; and lastly, the
requisitions of bequest.

513. Si plura sunt debita, vel plus legatum fuerit, ad quæ catalla defuncti
non sufficiant, fiat ubique defalcatio, excepto regis privilegio.
     If there should be more due, or more legacies bequeathed, than the
chattels of the deceased are sufficient to satisfy, let an equal abatement be
made on all the legacies, the privilege of the king being excepted.

513. Per mis.   In half.

513. Per mis et per tout.   In half and in all.

513. Probabilis causa litigandi.   A probable cause of litigation.

513. Solvendum in futuro.   To be paid at a future period.

515. Vexatæ quæstiones.   The vexatious questions.

516. De commorientibus.   Concerning persons dying together.

517. Collatio bonorum.   Equalizing the estates or goods.

520. Præfectus prætorii.   Judge of the court.

APPENDIX.

1.

VETUS CARTA FEOFFAMENTI.

SCIANT presentes et futuri, quod ego Willielmus, filius   PREMISES.
Willielmi de Segenho, dedi, concessi. et hac presenti carta mea
confirmavi, Johanni quondam filio Johannis de Saleford, pro
quadam summa pecunie quam mihi dedit pre manibus, unam
acram terre mee arabilis, jacentem in campo de Saleford, juxta
terram quondam Richardi de la Mere; Habendam et Tenen-   HABENDUM
dam totam predictam acram terre cum omnibus ejus pertinen-   &
tiis, prefato Johanni, et heredibus suis, et suis assignatis, de   TENENDUM.
capitalibus dominis feodi: Reddendo et faciendo annuatim   REDDENDUM.
eisdem dominis capitalibus servitia inde debita et consueta:
Et ego predictus Willielmus, et heredes mei, et mei assignati,   WARRANTY.
totam predictam acram terre, cum omnibus suis pertinentiis,
predicto Johanni de Saleford, et heredibus suis, et suis assignatis, contra omnes gentes warrantizabimus in perpetuum. In   CONCLUSION.
cujus rei testimonium huic presenti carte sigillum meum ap-
posui; Hiis testibus, Nigello de Saleford, Johanne de Seybroke,
Radulpho, clerico de Saleford, Johanne, molendario de eadem
villa, et aliis. Data apud Saleford die Veneris proximo ante
festum sancte Margarete virginis, anno regni regis Edwardi filii
regis Edwardi sexto.

(L. S.)

MEMORANDUM, quod die et anno infrascriptis plena et pacifica   LIVERY OF
seisina acre infraspecificate, cum pertinentiis, data et deliberata   SEISIN
fuit per infranominatum Willielmum de Segenho infranomi-   ENDORSED.
nato Johanni de Saleford, in propriis personis suis, secundum
tenorem et effectum carte infrascripte, in presentia Nigelli de
Saleford, Johannis de Seybroke, et aliorum.

AN OLD DEED OF FEOFFMENT.

KNOW all men present and to come, That I, William,   PREMISES.
son of William de Segenho, have given and granted, and by
this my present deed have confirmed, to John, son of John of
Saleford, for a certain sum of money which he has paid into
my hands, one acre of my arable land, lying in the plain of
Saleford, adjoining to the land of Richard de la Mere; To HAVE   HABENDUM
AND TO HOLD all the aforesaid acre of land, with all its appur-   AND
tenances, to the aforesaid John, and his heirs and assigns, of   TENENDUM.
the chief lords of the fee: Rendering and performing yearly to   REDDENDUM.
the same chief lords the services therefore due and accustomed: And I, the aforesaid William, and my heirs and   WARRANTY.
assigns, warrant all the aforesaid acre of land with all its appurtenances, to the aforesaid John of Saleford and to his heirs
and assigns, against all the world forever. In witness whereof   CONCLUSION.

I have put my seal to this present deed. Witness, Nigell de Saleford, John of Seybroke, Radulphus, clerk of Saleford, John, miller of the same town, and others. Given at Saleford, on the Friday next before the feast of St. Margaret the Virgin, in the sixth year of the reign of King Edward, the son of King Edward.

(L. S.)

LIVERY OF SEISIN ENDORSED.

MEMORANDUM, That on the day and year within written full and quiet seisin of the within specified acre, with its appurtenances, was given and delivered by the within named William de Segenho to the within named John of Saleford, in their own proper persons, according to the tenor and effect of the within written deed, in the presence of Nigell de Saleford, John of Seybroke, and others.

A

TRANSLATION,

&c., &c.

VOLUME THE THIRD.

For that which is without remedy, is by that very circumstance strengthened, if it be free from fault.

26. Procuratoribus, qui in aliquibus partibus attornati nuncupantur.
Proctors, who are in some places called attornies.

26. Cum olim in usu fuisset, alterius nomine agi non posse; sed, quia hoc non minimam incommoditatem habebat, cœperunt homines per procuratores litigare.
Although formerly it had been the custom for no one to act in the name of another; yet, as this was attended with great inconvenience, men began to carry on law-suits by proctors.

26.	Assumpsit.	He undertook.

26.	Quo tempore magna tranquillitas regnabat.	

At which time great tranquillity reigned.

26.	Apprenticii ad legem.	Apprentices to the law.

27.	Servientes ad legem.	Serjeants at law.

27.	Honoris causa.	As a mark of honor.

27. S'aggiungea, che coloro, che sapevan ben aringare, avean un gran vantaggio nell' assemblee del popolo, il quale si mena volontieri per l' orecchie; onde avviene che nello stato popolare gli avvocati sono ordinariamente quegli, chi hanno più potenza, ed autorita.
It was added, that good orators had a great advantage in the assembly of the people, who willingly suffer themselves to be captivated by sound; whence it arises, that in a popular state, advocates generally possess the greatest power and authority.

29.	Ferro in domo ejus incubuit.	He went home and fell upon his sword.

29. Qua cavetur antiquitus, nequis ob causam orandum pecuniam donumve accipiat.
By which it was anciently provided, that no one should receive money or presents for pleading a cause.

29. Capiendis pecuniis posuit modum, usque ad dena sestertia, quem egressi repetundarum tenerentur.
He fixed the amount of the sum to be received at ten thousand sesterces, to exceed which was considered as bribery.

29. Neequidquam publicæ mercis tam venale fuit quam advocatorum perfidia.
Nor was there any public traffic so venal as the perfidy of advocates.

29.   Quid enim est jus civile? quod neque inflecti gratia, neque perfringi potentia, neque adulterari pecunia possit.

For what is the civil law? that which can neither be biassed by favor, violated by power, nor corrupted by money.

---

32.   Curia pedis pulverizati.   The dusty-foot court.

---

34.   Pares.   Peers or equals.

---

34.   Quia tollit atque eximit causam e curia baronum.

Because it tolls, i. e. takes away and removes the cause from the court baron.

---

34.   Accedas ad curiam.   You may come to the court.

---

34.   Recordari facias loquelam.   That you cause the plaint to be recorded.

---

35.   Centeni ex singulis sunt, &c. [Vide ante, vol. i. p. 116.]

---

35.   Inter suos jus dicunt controversiasque minuunt.

Declare the law among their dependants, and abate controversies.

---

35.   Eliguntur in consiliis et principes, qui jura per pagos vicosque reddunt: centeni singulis, ex plebe comites, consilium simul et auctoritas adsunt.

The lords are also chosen in their councils who administer justice through the towns and districts. The jury for each hundred are chosen from the people, and have both council and authority.

36.   Forum plebeiæ justiciæ et theatrum comitivæ potestatis.

The court of justice for the common people and the theatre of the power of the county.

---

36.   In foro legis.   In a court of law.

---

36.   In foro conscientiæ.   In a court of conscience.

---

36.   Νομοθέται.   Promulgators of the law.

---

36.   Carmen necessarium.   An indispensable lesson.

---

36.   Mala in se.   Crimes in themselves.

---

36.   Mala prohibita.   Crimes, because forbidden.

---

37   Præpositus ad quartam circiter septimanam frequentem populi concionem celebrato: cuique jus dicito; litesque singulas dirimito.

Let the sheriff hold a full assembly of the people about once a month:

declare the law to every one; and severally determine suits.

---

38. Aula regia — Aula regis.   The King's Bench.

---

38. Capitalis justiciarius totius Angliæ.   Chief Justiciary of all England.

---

39. Communia placita non sequantur curiam regis, sed teneantur in aliquo loco certo.

Let not the common pleas follow the king's court, but be held in some fixed place.

---

41. Puisne.   Younger.

---

41. Nec super eos, per vim vel per arma ibimus nisi per legem regni nostri vel per judicium parium suorum.

Nor will we proceed against them by force or arms, unless warranted by the law of our kingdom, or by the judgment of their peers.

---

41. Coram ipso rege.   Before the king himself.

---

41. In curia domini regis ipse in propria persona jura decernit.

The king in person judges in his own court.

---

42. Ubicunque fuerimus in Anglia.

In whatever part of England we shall be.

---

42. Capitales, generales, perpetui, et majores; a latere regis residentes, qui omnium aliorum corrigere tenentur injurias et errores.

Chief, general, perpetual, and elder; accompanying the king, who are appointed to redress the injuries and correct the errors of all others.

---

42. In pari materia.   On the same subject matter.

---

43. Contra fictionem non admittitur probatio: quid enim efficeret probatio veritatis, ubi fictio adversus veritatem fingit? Nam fictio nihil aliud est, quam legis adversus veritatem in re possibili ex justa causa dispositio.

Proof is not admitted to contradict a fiction: for what would the proof of truth avail, where fiction counterfeits truth? For fiction is simply a supposition by the law, for a just cause, of something possible which is contrary to the truth.

---

43. In fictione juris semper subsistit æquitas.

A fiction of law is always founded in equity.

---

43. Dernier resort.   The last resort.

---

43. Inanissima prudentiæ et stultitiæ plenissima.

Entirely destitute of prudence and completely foolish.

45. Jura regalia.   Regal rights.

---

45. Jura fiscalia.   Fiscal rights.

---

46. Quo minus sufficiens existit.   Whereby he is less able.

---

46. Articuli super cartas.   Articles on the charters.

---

48. Valor beneficiorum.   The value of benefices.

---

48. Del tax de vint mares et dedeyns.
Of the rate of twenty marks and under.

48. Ultra taxam viginti marcarum usque ad taxam triginta marcarum inclusive.

Beyond the rate of twenty marks to the rate of thirty marks inclusive.

---

48. Virtute officii sui.   By virtue of his office.

---

48. Inclusive.   Inclusively.

---

48. Usque ad triginta.   To thirty.

48. De primo beneficio ecclesiastico habendo. Volumus quod idem A. ad primum beneficium ecclesiasticum (taxationem viginti marcarum excedens) vacaturum, quod ad præsentionem nostram pertinuerit, &c.

Of possessing the first ecclesiastical benefice. We will that the same A. be presented to the first vacant ecclesiastical benefice (exceeding the rate of twenty marks) which shall be in our presentation.

---

48. Toutz esglises que passent l'extent de 20 mares.
All churches which exceed the amount of twenty marks.

---

48. Monstrans de droit.   Showing of right.

---

49. Propria manu.   With his own hand.

---

49. Officina justitiæ.   The magazine of justice.

---

49. Ex debito justitiæ.   As due to justice.

50. Jam illis promissis non esse standum, quis non videt, quæ coactus quis metu et deceptus dolo promiserit? quæ quidem plerumque jure prætorio liberantur, nonnulla legibus.

To whom is it not evident that promises made through fear or fraud are of no validity? some of which are dissolved at the discretion of the judge, and some by the laws.

51. Nemo ad regem appellet pro aliqua lite, nisi jus domi consequi non possit. Si jus nimis severum fit, alleviatio deinde quæratur apud regem.

No one may appeal to the king in any suit, unless he cannot obtain justice at home. If the decision be too severe, then a mitigation of it may be prayed from the king.

---

51.   Hic est, qui leges regni cancellat iniquas,
       Et mandata pii principis æqua facit.

It is he who cancels the unequitable laws of the kingdom, and executes the just mandates of a righteous prince.

---

52. Le subpœna ne serroit my cy soventement use come il est ore, si nous attendomus tiels actions sur les cases, et mainteinomus le jurisdiction de ceo court, et d'auter courts.

The subpœna would not be so often used here as it now is, if we were to pay attention to actions on the case, and maintain the jurisdiction of this and other courts.

---

52. Pro læsione fidei.   For a breach of faith.

---

52. Placita de debitis, quæ fide interposita debentur, vel absque interpositione fidei, sint in justitia regis.

Let those pleas of debts, which are due with or without the interposition of a trust, be in the king's jurisdiction.

---

59. Justiciarii itinerantes venerunt apud Wigorniam in octavis S. Johannis baptistæ; et totus comitatus eos admittere recusavit, quod septem anni nondum erant elapsi, postquam justiciarii ibidem ultimo sederunt.

The itinerant justices came to the city of Worcester on the octave of St. John the Baptist; but the whole county refused to admit them because seven years had not yet elapsed since the justices had last sat there.

---

59. Justiciarii ad omnia placita.   Justices for all pleas.

---

59. Si non omnes.   If not all.

---

60. Oyer et terminer.   To hear and determine.

---

61. Celeberrimo huic conventui episcopus et aldermannus inter sunto; quorum alter jura divina, alter humana populum edoceto.

Let the bishop and alderman be present at this illustrious assembly; of whom let the one instruct the people in divine, the other in human laws.

---

62. Sacerdotes a regibus honorandi sunt, non judicandi.
Priests are to be honored, not judged, by kings.

---

62. Ite et inter vos causas vestras discutite, quia dignum non est ut nos judicemus Deos.

Go and discuss your causes among yourselves, for it is not fit that we should judge Gods.

63. Nullus episcopus vel archidiaconus de legibus episcopalibus amplius in hundret placita teneant, nec causam, quæ ad regimen animarum pertinet ad judicium secularium hominum adducant: sed quicunque secundum episcopales leges, de quacunque causa vel culpa interpellatus fuerit, ad locum, quem ad hoc episcopus elegerit et nominaverit, veniat; ibique de causa sua respondeat; et non secundum hundret, sed secundum canones et episcopales leges, rectum Deo et episcopo suo faciat.

No bishop or archdeacon shall longer hold pleas in the hundred court that are to be decided by episcopal laws, nor bring any cause which relates to spiritual matters [the government of souls] for the judgment of secular persons; but whoever shall be sued according to the episcopal laws, for any cause or offence, shall come to the place chosen and appointed by the bishop for that purpose, and there make his own defence; to the end that right may be done to God and his bishop, according to the canon and episcopal laws, and not those of the hundred.

---

63. Volo et præcipio, ut omnes de comitatu eant ad comitatus et hundreda, sicut fecerint tempore regis Edwardi.

I will and command that all persons belonging to the county attend the county and hundred courts as they did in the time of king Edward.

---

63. Generalia comitatuum placita certis locis et vicibus teneantur. Intersint autem episcopi, comites, &c. et agantur primo debita veræ christianitatis jura, secundo regis placita, postremo causæ singulorum dignis satisfactionibus expleantur.

Let the general pleas of the counties be held in certain places and districts; and the bishops and counts, &c. be present; and first, let all affairs concerning religion be transacted; next, the pleas of the crown; and lastly, let the causes of individuals be heard and justly determined.

---

63. Ne episcopi secularium placitorum officium suscipiant.
Let no bishop take charge of secular pleas.

---

65. Bona notabilia.
Goods of a person to the value of a hundred shillings, lying in another house than that in which he died, and hereby rendered cognizable by probate before the archbishop of the province, unless by special custom it be otherwise.

---

66. Judices delegati.	Delegated judges.

---

71. De viridi et venatione.	Of vert and venison.

---

72. De super-oneratione forestariorum et aliorum ministrorum forestæ; et de eorum oppressionibus populo regis illatis.

Concerning the impositions of the foresters, and other officers of the forest; and their oppression on the king's people.

---

73. Pro re nata. According to circumstances—For the occasion.

76. Supersedeas.
A command to stay or forbear doing that which ought not to be done.

77. Certiorari.   To have notice given him.

77. Latitat.   He lies concealed.

78. Breve domini regis non currit. The king's writ does not run.

85. Sui.   Of himself.

88. Si rector petat versus parochianos oblationes et decimas debitas et consuetas.
If the rector sue his parishioners for oblations and tithes due and accustomed.

89. Circumspecte agatis.   That ye act cautiously.

91. Indicavit.   '   He showed.

94. In facie ecclesiae.   In the face of the church.

94. Ex post facto.   After the fact.

94. A mensa et thoro.   From bed and board.

94. In fraudem legis.   Unlawfully.

95. De consuetudine Angliæ, et super consensu regio et suorum procerum in talibus ab antiquo concesso.
By the custom of England, and the consent of the king and his nobles anciently granted in such cases.

95. Ab olim.   Formerly.

95. Consensu regis et magnatum regni Angliæ.
By the command of the king and the peers of the kingdom of England.

95. Olim a prælatis cum approbatione regis et baronum dicitur emanasse.
Is said to have emanated formerly from the prelates with the approbation of the king and barons.

95. Non nullam habebant episcopi authoritatem, præter eam quam a rege acceptam referebant. Jus testamenta probandi non habebant: administrationis potestatem cuique delegare non poterant.
The bishops had no other authority than what they received from the king. They had not the right of proving wills; neither could they grant the power of administration.

96. Cujus regis temporibus hoc ordinatum sit, non reperio.
I do not find in what king's reign this was ordained.

96. Ab antiquo. Anciently.

96. Ab olim ordinatum. Ordained formerly.

96. Per visum ecclesiæ. Under the direction of the church.

96. Quod distributio rerum quæ in testamento relinquuntur auctoritate ecclesiæ fiet.
That a distribution of the things which are left by will, be made by the authority of the church.

96. Si quis aliquid dixerit contra testamentum, placitum illud in curia christianitatis audiri debet et terminari.
If any thing be averred against a will, that plea should be heard and determined in the spiritual court.

97. Magister census. An officer for taking the value of estates.

97. Absurdum etenim clericis est, immo etiam opprobriosum, si peritos se velint ostendere disceptationum esse forensium.
For it is absurd, nay more, it is disgraceful for clergymen to wish to display their skill in forensic disputes.

97. Quæ secundum canones et episcopales leges ad regimen animarum pertinuit.
Which belonged, according to the canon and episcopal laws, to spiritual matters.

97. Si quis baronum seu hominum meorum pecuniam suam non dederit vel dare dis posuerit, uxor sua, sive liberi, aut parentes et legitimi homines ejus, eam pro anima ejus dividant sicut eis melius visum fuerit.
If any one of my barons or vassals shall not have disposed of his wealth, or directed the disposal of it, let his wife, children, or parents and proper persons divide it, for the good of his soul, as shall seem best to them.

97. Pro salute animæ ejus, ecclesiæ consilio.
For the good of his soul, by the advice and direction of the church.

100. De contumace capiendo. For taking the contumacious.

101. De excommunicato capiendo. For taking the excommunicated.

102. In numero impiorum ac sceleratorum habentur: ab iis omnes decedunt, aditum eorum sermonemque defugiunt, ne quid ex contagione incommodi accipiant: neque iis potentibus jus redditur, neque honos ullus communicatur.

Are reckoned among the impious and wicked: all shun them, fly their approach, and avoid all communication with them, lest they receive some injury from the contagion: neither is justice rendered to them when they seek it, nor is any honor conferred on them.

102. Probus et legalis homo. A true and lawful man.

102. Significavit. He signified.

102. De excommunicato deliberando.
For liberating the excommunicated.

102. Si aliquis per superbiam elatus ad justitiam episcopalem venire noluerit, vocetur semel, secundo, et tertio: quod si nec sic ad emendationem venerit, excommunicetur; et, si opus fuerit, ad hoc vindicandum fortitudo et justitia regis sive vicecomitis adhibeatur.

If any one, elate with pride, come not to the episcopal court, let him be summoned three times, and if he attend not then its due correction, let him be excommunicated; and, if necessary, let the power and justice of the king, or sheriff, be exerted to punish his contempt.

103. Nullum tempus occurrit ecclesiæ. No time runs against the church.

106. Post mortem. After death.

107. Lex cornelia. The Cornelian law.

109. Procedendo ad judicium. For proceeding to judgment.

111. Coram non judice.
Before a judge unauthorized to take cognizance of the affair.

113. Ad aliud examen. To another examination or trial.

116. Jus prosequendi in judicio quod alicui debetur.
The right of prosecuting to judgment which is due to every one.

116. Actiones compositæ sunt, quibus inter se homines disceptarent: quas actiones, ne populus prout vellet institueret, certas solemnesque esse voluerunt.

Forms of process were settled, by which men might argue their differences, which forms were established and made certain, that the people might not at pleasure institute their own modes of proceeding.

117. Sunt jura, sunt formulæ, de omnibus rebus constitutæ, ne quis aut in genere injuriæ aut in ratione actionis, errare possit. Expressæ enim sunt ex uniuscujusque damno, dolore, incommodo, calamitate, injuria, publicæ a prætore formulæ, ad quas privata lis accommodatur.

There are rights, there are forms appointed for all things, lest any one should mistake either the kind of injury or the mode of redress. For public forms are composed by the prætor from every species of loss, trouble, inconvenience, calamity, and injury, for the accommodation of private suits.

117. Sunt quædam brevia formata super certis casibus de cursu, et de communi consilio totius regni approbata et concessa, quæ quidem nullatenus mutari poterint absque consensu et voluntate eorum.

There are some writs formed on certain cases, granted and approved by the common council of the kingdom, which can in no wise be changed without its will and consent.

117. Actiones in personam, quæ adversus eum intenduntur, qui ex contractu vel delicto obligatus est aliquid dare vel concedere.

Personal actions which are commenced against him who by contract, or through the commission of some offence, is bound to give or surrender something.

120. De injuriis.	Of injuries.
121. Super visum vulneris.	On view of the wound.
122. Mala praxis.	Bad practice.

122 Culpæ adnumerantur, veluti si medicus curationem dereliquerit, male quempiam secuerit, aut perperam ei medicamentum dederit.

They are reckoned faults, as if a medical man neglect his patient, perform an amputation unskillfully, or administer medicine unadvisedly.

122. Rex vicecomiti salutem. Si A. fecerit te securum de clamore suo prosequendo tunc pone per vadium et salvos plegios B. quod sit coram justiciariis nostris apud Westmonasterium in Octavis Sancti Michaelis ostensurus quare cum idem B. ad dextrum oculum ipsius A. casualiter læsum bene et competenter curandum apud S. pro quadam pecuniæ summa præ manibus soluta assumpsisset, idem B. curam suam circa oculum prædictum tam negligenter et improvide apposuit, quod idem A. defectu ipsius B. visum oculi prædicti totaliter amisit ad damnum ipsius A. viginti librarum, ut dicit. Et habeas ibi nomina plegiorum et hoc breve. Teste meipso apud Westmonasterium, &c.

The king to the sheriff sends greeting. If A. give you security that he will prosecute his claim, then put B. by gage and safe pledges to appear before our justices at Westminster on the octave of St. Michael, to show cause why, when the same B. had at S. undertaken, for a certain sum of money paid beforehand, well and completely to cure the right eye of the said A. accidentally hurt, the same B. attended to the said eye so negligently and carelessly, that the same A., by the default of the same B., totally lost the sight of the said eye, to the damage of the said A. (as he says) of twenty pounds. And have you there the names of the pledges and this writ. Witness myself at Westminster, &c.

123. Vi et armis.   By force and arms.

123. Scandalum magnatum.   Slander of the nobles.

125. Damnum absque injuria.   Damage without injury.

125. Eum qui nocentem infamat, non est æquum et bonum ob eam rem condemnari; delicta enim nocentium nota esse oportet et expedit.

It is not just and right that he who exposes the faults of a guilty person should be condemned on that account; for it is proper and expedient that the offences of the guilty should be known.

128. De odio et atia.   Of hatred and ill-will.

128. De homine replegiando.   Of replevying a man.

129. Capias in withernam.   That you take in withernam.

129. Nisi captus est per speciale præceptum nostrum, vel capitalis justiciarii nostri, vel pro morte hominis, vel pro foresta nostra, vel pro aliquo alio retto quare secundum consuetudinem Angliæ non sit replegiabilis.

Unless he be taken by our special command, or by that of our chief justice, for the death of a man, for a breach of the forest laws, or any other offence for which, according to the custom of England, he may not be repleviable.

129. Habeas corpus ad respondendum.
That you have the body to answer.

129. Ad satisfaciendum.   To satisfy.

130. Ad prosequendum, testificandum, deliberandum, &c.
To prosecute, testify, deliberate, &c.

130. Habeas corpus ad testificandum.
That you have the body for a witness.

130. Ad faciendum et recipiendum.   To do and receive.

130. Habeas corpus cum causa.
That you have the body with the cause of detention.

131. Die Jovis prox. post quinden. Sancti Martini.
The Thursday next after the quindena [Nov. 25] of St. Martin.

134. Etiam judicum tunc primarius, nisi illud faceremus, rescripti illius forensis, qui libertatis personalis omnimodæ vindex legitimus est fere solus, usum omnimodum palam pronuntiavit (sui semper similis) nobis perpetuo in posterum denegandum. (Quod, ut odiosissimum juris prodigium, scientioribus hic universis censitum.

Then also the chief justice (always the same) openly declared, that unless we could do it [find sureties for good behavior] the use of this forensic rescript, which is almost the only lawful protection of every kind of personal liberty, would ever after be denied us. Which was considered by all the lawyers present as a most odious and monstrous declaration.

137. Habeas corpus ad subjiciendum. That you have the body to answer.

139. De uxore rapta et abducta.
For the ravishment and abduction of his wife.

140. Volenti non fit injuria.   The willing receive no injury.

140. Particeps criminis.   A partaker of the crime.

140. Per quod consortium amisit.   By which means he lost his wife.

141. Mutatis mutandis.
Being varied according to the circumstances of the case.

141. De filio vel filia rapta vel abducta.
For the ravishment or abduction of the son or daughter.

141. De custodia terræ et hæredis.   For the custody of the land and heir.

142. Per quod servitium amisit.   By which means he lost his service.

142. In loco parentis.   In the place of a parent.

142. Secundum allegata et probata.
According to what had been alleged and proved.

146. Replegiare est, rem apud alium detentam cautione legitima interposita, redimere.
Replevin is to redeem, with lawful security, any thing detained by another.

146. Quant les biens ou chattels d'aucun sont prises, il avera per common ley un breve hors de chancery commandant, &c.
When the goods or chattels of a man are taken, he shall have a writ out of chancery, by the common law, commanding, &c.

146. Lex neminem cogit ad vana seu impossibilia.
The law compels no one to do things which are either useless or impossible.

147. Replegiari facias.   That you cause to be replevied.

147. Plegios de retorno habendo.   Pledges to have the return.

148. Recordari facias loquelam.
That you cause the complaint to be recorded.

148. De proprietate probanda.	For proving the ownership.
151. Animo furandi.	With a design of stealing them.
152. Detinue de biens.	Detaining of goods.
153. Indebitatus assumpsit.	Being indebted he undertook.
153. Pro tanto.	For so much.
156. Debet et detinet.	He owes and detains.
157. Toties quoties.	As often as — As often so often.
157. Finalis concordia.	Final agreement.
158. Nudum pactum.	A barren contract.

161. Prochein amy.   Next friend — next of kin to the infant.

162. Qui tam pro domino rege, &c. quam pro se ipso in hac parte sequitur.
Who prosecutes this suit as well for the king, &c. as for himself.

163. Quantum valebat.	As much as it was worth.
163. Ex æquo et bono.	By equity and right.

163. In pari delicto potior est conditio defendentis.
Where the fault is equal on both sides the defendant is in the best condition.

163. Assumpsit.	He undertook.
165. In toto.	In the whole — Entirely.
173. Propter defectum sanguinis.	Through failure of issue.
176. Ad terminum qui præteriit.	For the term which has passed.
176. Jus proprietatis.	Right of property.
176. Jus possessionis.	Right of possession.
176. In statu quo.	In its original state.
178. Non compos mentis.	Of unsound mind.

179. Manu forti.   With a strong hand.

181. Non habuit ingressum nisi per intrusionem quam ipse fecit.
He had no entry but by the intrusion which he himself made.

181. Non habuit ingressum, nisi per Gulielmum qui se in illud intrusit, et illud tenenti dimisit.
He had no entry but through William who intruded himself on it, and demised it to the tenant.

181. Non habuit ingressum, nisi per Ricardum, cui Gulielmus illud dimisit, cui se in illud intrusit.
He had no entry but through Richard, to whom William, who had intruded on the land, demised it.

182. Non habuit ingressum nisi post intrusionem quam Gulielmus in illud fecit.
He had no entrance but after the intrusion which William made on it.

182. Sur disseisin.   On disseisin.

183. Unde nihil habet.   Whereby she has nothing.

183. Dum fuit infra ætatem.   While he was under age.

183. Dum fuit non compos mentis.   While he was of unsound mind.

183. Cui in vita.   Whom in his lifetime.

183. Cui ante divortium   Whom before divorce.

183. Cui in vita sua, vel cui ante divortium, ipsa contradicere non potuit.
Whom in his lifetime, or whom before divorce, she could not contradict.

183. Ad communem legem.   At common law.

183. In casu proviso.   In the case provided.

183. In consimili casu.   In the like case.

183. Causa matrimonii prælocuti.
In consideration of a marriage before agreed on.

183. Registrum omnium brevium.   A register of all writs.

184. Festinum remedium.   The speedy remedy.

184. Mort d'ancestor.   Death of the ancestor.

184. Novel disseisin.   New disseisin.

---

185. Si dominus feodi negat hæredibus defuncti saisinam ejusdem feodi, justitiarii domini regis faciant inde fieri recognitionem per xii legales homines, qualem saisinam defunctus inde habuit, die qua fuit vivus et mortuus; et sicut recognitum fuerit, ita hæredibus ejus restituant. S. 10. Justitiarii domini regis faciant fieri recognitionem de dissaisinis factis super assisam, a tempore quo dominus rex venit in Angliam proxime post pacem factam inter ipsum et regem filium suum.

If the lord of the fee refuse to the heirs of the deceased seisin of the same fee, the king's justices may cause an inquiry to be made by twelve lawful men, of what seisin the deceased had on the day of his death, and according to the result of such inquiry it shall be restored to his heirs. S. 10. The king's justices shall cause an inquiry to be made of the disseisins made upon assize, from the time at which the king came into England, next after the peace made between him and his son.

---

186. De avo.   From the grandfather.

---

186. De proavo.   From the great grandfather.

---

186. Nuper obiit.   He lately died.

---

187. De assis. mortis antecessoris.
Concerning the assize of the death of the ancestor.

---

187. Nul tort, nul disseisin. ‘   No wrong, no disseisin.

---

188. Talis qui ita convictus fuerit, dupliciter delinquit contra regem: quia facit disseisinam et roberiam contra pacem suam; et etiam ausu temerario irrita facit ea, quæ in curia domini regis rite acta sunt: et propter duplex delictum merito sustinere debet pœnam duplicatam.

He who is so convicted offends doubly against the king; first, because he makes a disseisin and robbery against his peace; and secondly, by a rash undertaking sets at defiance the just decisions of the king's court: and for this double offence he deserves a double punishment.

---

188. Nam leges vigilantibus, non dormientibus, subveniunt.
For the laws aid the vigilant, not the careless.

---

190. Jus et seisinam.   A right and seisin.

---

190. Juris et seisinam conjunctionem. The conjunction of right and seisin.

---

191. Secundum formam doni.   According to the form of the gift.

---

193. Quod ei deforceat.   That he deforced him.

---

194. De rationabili parte.   For the reasonable part.

195. Præcipe in capite.   Command for the tenant in capite.

195. Quia dominus remisit curiam.   Because the lord has waived his court.

195. Secundum consuetudinem manerii.
According to the custom of the manor.

195. Pone.   Put.

195. Tenir en socage.   To hold in socage.

195. Garde.   Wardship.

195. Briefe de recto claus.   Writ of right close.

195. Recordari facias.   That you cause to be recorded.

198. Elegit.   He hath chosen.

199. De mercatoribus.   Of merchants.

199. Ut liberum tenementum.   As a freehold.

199. Ejectione firmæ.   Of ejection of farm.

199. Quare ejecit infra terminum.   Why he hath ejected within the term.

200. Ejectione firmæ n'est que un action de trespass en son nature, et le plaintiff ne recovera son terme que est a venir, nient plus que en trespas home recovera damages pur trespass nient fait, mes a feser; mais il convient a suer par action de covenant ad comen law a recoverer son terme; quod tota curia concessit. Et per Belknap, la comen ley est, lou home est ouste de son terme par estranger, il avera ejectione firmæ versus cesty que luy ouste; et sil soit ouste par son lessor, briefe de covenant; et sil par lessee ou grantee de reversion, briefe de covenant versus son lessor, et countera especial count, &c.

A writ of EJECTIONE FIRMÆ is in its nature merely an action of trespass, and the plaintiff shall only recover that part of the term which is unexpired, the same as in trespass, a man shall recover no damages for a trespass not committed but to be committed. But to recover his term he must sue by an action of covenant at common law; to which the whole court assented. And per Belknap; where a man is ousted from his term by a stranger, the common law is, that he shall have a writ of EJECTIONE FIRMÆ against him who ousted him; and if he be ousted by his lessor, a writ of covenant; and if by the lessee, or grantee of the reversion, a writ of covenant against his lessor, and he shall count a special count, &c.

201. Si home port EJECTIONE FIRMÆ, le plaintiff recovera son terme qui est arrere, si bien come in QUARE EJECIT INFRA TERMINUM; et, si nul soit arrere, donques tout in damages.

If a plaintiff bring a writ of EJECTIONE FIRMÆ he shall recover the remainder of his term as well as in a QUARE EJECIT INFRA TERMINUM, and, if it be all run out, he shall recover the whole in damages.

209. Vi et armis.	By force and arms.
209. Quare clausum fregit.	Wherefore he broke his close.
209. Meum et tuum.	Mine and thine.

209. Qui alienum fundum ingreditur, potest a domino, si is præviderit, prohiberi ne ingrediatur.

He who enters on another's land may be resisted by the owner if he shall have previously forbidden it.

210. Quantum.	Quantity.
210. Jus postliminii.	Remitter.
210. Jure uxoris.	In right of his wife.
211. In foro contentioso.	In a court of litigation.

211. Quare vi et armis clausum ipsius A. apud B. fregit, et blada ipsius A. ad valentiam centum solidorum ibidem nuper crescentia cum quibusdam averiis depastus fuit, conculcavit et consumpsit, &c.

Wherefore he broke the close of the said A. at B. by force and arms, razed, trampled on, and consumed the grass of the said A. lately growing thereon, with certain beasts to the value of twenty shillings, &c.

212. Continuando.	By continuation.
213. Ab initio.	From the beginning.
214. Inter alia.	Among other things.

217. Sic utere tuo ut alienum non lædas.
So use your property that you do not injure that of another.

217. Cujus est solum, &c. [Vide ante, vol. ii., p. 18.]

219. Damnum absque injuria.	Damage without injury.
220. Quod permittat posternere.	That he permit to abate or put down.
221. Ad nocumentum liberi tenementi sui.	To the damage of his freehold.
221. In casu consimili.	In a similar case.

221. De cætero non recedant querentes a curia domini regis, pro eo quod tenementum transfertur de uno in alium.

Moreover the complainants shall not be obliged to abandon their action because the tenement is transferred to another.

---

221. Quod A. injuste levavit tale nocumentum.
That A. unjustly levied such a nuisance.

---

221. Quod A. et B. levaverunt.	That A. and B. levied.

---

224. Nemo est hæres viventis.	No one is heir to the living.

---

224. Hæres natus.	Heir born, or natural heir.

---

224. Hæres factus.	Heir made or appointed.

---

224. Damnum.	Loss.

---

225. In esse.	In being.

---

225. Ad exhæredationem ipsius.	To his disherison.

---

225. Ad exhæredationem ecclesiæ.	To the disherison of the church.

---

225. Estrepement pendente placito.	Waste pending the suit.

---

226. Ne faciat vastum vel estrepementum pendente placito dicto indiscusso.

That he do not commit waste or devastation during the continuance of the suit.

---

227. Non fecit vastum contra prohibitionem.

That he did not commit waste against prohibition.

---

228. Nam de minimis non curat lex. For the law does not recognize trifles.

---

229. Fortuna ignis vel hujusmodi eventus inopinati omnes tenentes excusant.

The accident of fire, or unexpected events of that kind excuse all tenants.

---

230. Ratione tenuræ.	By reason of the tenure.

---

230. Commune vinculum.	Common bond.

---

231. Instar omnium.	Equal to all.

232. De consuetudinibus et servitiis.   Of customs and services.

---

232. Cessavit.	He hath ceased.

232. Eo quod tenens in faciendis servitiis per biennium jam cessavit.
Because the tenant has already ceased to do service for two years.

---

232. Per totum triennium.   For three whole years.

---

233. Sur disclaimer.   On disclaimer.

---

234. Vasallus, qui abnegavit feudum ejusve conditionem, exspoliabitur.
The vassal who has denied either his fee, or the condition by which he held it, shall be deprived of it.

---

234. Ne injuste vexes.   Do not unjustly oppress.

---

235. A sequendo.   From following.

---

235. De secta ad molendinum.   For suit at his mill.

---

235. Quam ad illud facere debet, et solet.
Which he ought, and was used to do at it.

---

235. Secta ad furnum, secta ad torrale, et ad omnia hujusmodi.
His suit at the oven, his suit at the kiln, and all others of the same kind.

---

237. Per quod.   By which.

---

239. Levant et couchant.
Rising up and lying down: i. e. when cattle have been long enough on a man's ground to lie down and rise up again to feed.

---

240. Quod permittat.   That he permit.

---

243. Pro hac vice.   For this turn.

---

245. Darrein presentment.   Last presentation.

---

245. Quare impedit.   Wherefore he has hindered.

---

246. Caveat.   That he take care.

---

246. Jus patronatus.   Right of advowson.

---

247. Duplex querela.   A double complaint.

---

248. Ne admittas.   Do not admit.

---

248. Quare incumbravit.   Wherefore he has encumbered.

---

249. Infra tempus semestre.   Within half a year.

250. Pendente lite.	Pending the suit.
250. Ad admittendum clericum.	For admitting the clerk.
250. Quare non admisit.	Why he has not admitted.
250. Juris utrum.	To which of the two the right belongs.

257. Quod manus domini regis amoveantur et possessio restituatur petenti, salvo jure domini regis.

That the hand of the king be removed, and possession restored to the petitioner, saving the right of the king.

258. Virtute officii.	By virtue of their office.
258. A nativitate.	From his birth.
258. Inquisitio post mortem.	An inquest after death.
262. Quo warranto.	By what warrant.
264. In summo jure.	In strict right.
265. Mandamus.	We command.
265. In toto.	Entirely.

271 Forma et figura judicii.	The form and appearance of judgment.

273. Nulli vendemus, &c. [Vide ante, vol. i. p. 141.]

274. Si te fecerit securum.	If he give you security.

275. Nisi sub scriptura aut specificatione trium testium, quod actionem vellet prosequi.

Unless under writing, or the specification of three witnesses, that he will prosecute the action.

275. Dies fasti et nefasti.	Lawful and unlawful days.

276. De temporibus et diebus pacis.
Concerning the times and days of peace.

278. Illud ex libertate vitium, quod non simul nec jussi conveniunt, sed et alter et tertius dies cunctatione coeuntium absumitur.

There is this fault resulting from their liberty, that they come not together at the time appointed, but a second and a third day are lost by the delay of those who are to assemble.

278. Illud enim nimiæ libertatis indicium, concessa toties impunitas non parendi; nec enim trinis judicii concessibus pœnam perditæ causæ contumax meruit.

For the impunity with which they so often neglected to appear was a sign of their excessive liberty; nor were the contumacious punished by losing their cause, as three days grace was allowed.

279. In jus vocando.   By citing to justice.

280. Baculus nuntiatorius.   The nuntiatory staff.

281. Mittitur adversarius in possessionem bonorum ejus.
His adversary is put into possession of his goods.

281. Capias ad respondendum.   That you take him to answer.

281. Quare clausum fregit.   Why he hath broken his close.

283. In fictione juris equitas consistit.
All fiction of law is founded in equity.

283. Exigi facias.   That you cause to be required.

283. Quinto exactus.   Required for the fifth time.

284. Capias utlagatum.   That you take the outlaw.

284. Venditioni exponas.   That you expose for sale.

284. Scire facias.   That you make known.

284. Levari facias.   That you cause to be levied.

284. Amoveas manus.   That you remove the hand.

284. Ubicunque fuerimus in Anglia.
In whatever part of England we may be.

285. Oyer et terminer.   To hear and determine.

285. Latitat.   He lies hidden.

286. Venire facias ad respondendum.   That you cause to come to answer.

286. Distringas.   That you distrain.

286. Alias.   As formerly.

286. Pluries.   As more than once.

286 Capias.   That you take.
_____

287. In pari materia.   In like circumstances.
_____

288. Ac etiam.   And also.
_____

288. Cepi corpus.   I have taken the body.
_____

289. Eundo et redeundo.   In going and returning.
_____

291. Stipulatio et satisdatio.
A stipulation and putting in sufficient security.
_____

292. Exoneretur.   Let him be exonerated.
_____

292. Ad libitum.   At pleasure.
_____

293. Ore tenus.   By word of mouth.
_____

293. Viva voce.   By word of mouth.
_____

294. Certiorari.   To have notice given him.
_____

294. Scandalum magnatum.   Slander of the nobles.
_____

295. Ex delicto.   Arising from offence or misdeed.
_____

295. Ex contractu.   Arising from a contract.
_____

295. Quantum valebant.   As much as they were worth.
_____

296. Retraxit.   He hath withdrawn.
_____

297. Contestatio litis.   The opening of a case before witnesses.
_____

297. Jus prædicti S. et sœsinam ipsius.
The right and seisin of the aforesaid S.
_____

298. En la defense, &c. [translated in the text.]
_____

299. Jeo vous dirai un fable. En ascun temps fuit un pape, et avoit fait un grand offence, et le cardinals vindrent a luy et disoyent a luy "peccasti:" et il dit, "judica me:" et ils disoyent "non possumus, quia caput es ecclesiæ: judica teipsum:" et l'apostol dit, "judico me cremari;" et fuit combustus; et apres fuit un sainct. Et in ceo cas il fuit son juge demene, et issint n'est pas inconvenient qu'un home soit juge demene.

I will tell you a story. There was formerly a pope, and he committed a great crime, and the cardinals came to him, and said, "thou hast sinned:" and he said, "judge me:" and they answered, "we cannot, for thou art the head of the church; judge thyself:" and the apostle said, "I sentence myself to be burned;" and burned he was; and afterwards he was made a saint. And in that case he was his his own judge, and therefore it is not improper that a man should judge himself.

299. Licentia loquendi.   Liberty of speaking.

301. In rerum natura.   In the nature of things, or, in the world.

302. Ex delicto.   From wrong done.

302. Actio personalis moritur cum persona.
    A personal action dies with the person.

302. Ex contractu.   From contract.

304. Cognovit actionem.   He hath acknowledged the action.

304. Indebitatus assumpsit.   Being indebted, he undertook.

308. Interest reipublicæ ut sit finis litium.
    It is for the public good that there be an end to contentions.

308. Son assault demesne.   His own assault.

310. Exceptio, replicatio, duplicatio, triplicatio, et quadruplicatio.
    Exception, replication, duplication, triplication, and quadruplication.

315. Judices ordinarii.   Ordinary judges.

317. Audita querela.   The complaint has been heard.

318. Gallica causidicos docuit facunda Britannos.
    Eloquent Gaul hath instructed British lawyers.

318. Occidere, interficere, necare.   To kill, to put to death, to slay.

321. Fidei commissarios, cubiculum, filium familias, repudium, compromissum, reverentia et obsequium.
    Trustees, a bed-chamber, the son of a family, a divorce, a bond or engagement wherein two parties oblige themselves to stand to the arbitration or award of the umpire, reverence and compliance.

322. Materia prima.   The primary matter.

322. Neque quid, neque quantum, neque quale, neque aliquid eorum quibus ens determinatur.
    Neither that, nor as much as, nor such as, nor any part of those things by which being is determined.

322. Materia prima non est corpus, neque per formam corporeitatis, neque per simplicem essentiam: est tamen ens, et quidem substantia, licet incompleta; habetque actum ex se entitativum, et simul est potentia subjectiva.

Primary matter is not body, neither by form of corporeity nor by simple essence: nevertheless it is a being, and certain substance although incomplete; and has an entitative action from itself, and is at the same time a subjective power.

323. Ne per scripturam aliqua fiat in posterum dubitatio, jubemus non per siglorum captiones et compendiosa enigmata ejusdem codicis textum conscribi sed per literarum consequentiam explanari concedimus.

Lest, through the method of writing, the meaning of this code be rendered doubtful to posterity, we command that it be not written in abbreviations or ciphers; but that it be rendered plain by the regular succession of letters.

326. Sic volo, sic jubeo.	So I will, so I command.
329. Ex facto oritur jus.	Law arises from fact.
334. Ultra mare.	Beyond sea.

337. Novitas incognitæ disciplinæ, ut solita armis decerni jure terminarentur.

The introduction of a custom never before heard of; that matters which had always been decided by arms should be determined by law.

338. Non sine magna jurisconsultorum perturbatione.
Not without great disturbance of the lawyers.

340. Amittere liberam legem.	To lose his free law.
340. Liber et legalis homo.	A free and lawful man.

341. Est autem magna assisa regale quoddam beneficium, clementia principis, de consilio procerum, populis indultum; quo vitæ hominum, et status integritati tam salubriter consulitur, ut, retinendo quod quis possidet in libero tenemento soli, duelli casum declinare possint homines ambiguum. Ac per hoc contingit, insperatæ et prematuræ mortis ultimum evadere supplicium, vel saltem perennis infamiæ opprobrium illius infesti et inverecundi verbi, quod in ore victi turpiter sonat, consecutivum. Ex æquitate item maxima prodita est legalis ista institutio. Jus enim, quod post multas et longas dilationes vix evincitur per duellum, per beneficium istius constitutionis commodius et acceleratius expeditur.

The grand assize is a certain royal favor granted to the people by the clemency of the king, in counsel with his nobles: by which the lives and estates of men are so effectually consulted, that, every one retaining what he possesses in fee, may decline the doubtful event of the trial by battel: and by this means avoid the greatest of all punishments, an unexpected and premature death, or at least the disgrace and perpetual infamy attached to that base and odious word pronounced by the vanquished. This legal institution proceeds also from the highest equity: for the right which after many and long delays can scarcely be ascertained by battel, is, by this means, more commodiously and expeditiously determined.

342. Liberam legem.	Their free law.
343. De fidelitate.	On his fidelity.
343. De credulitate.	On their belief.
343. Jurabit duodecima manu.	He shall swear by twelve men.

343. Quod defendat se duodecima manu.
That he defend himself by twelve men.

343. Adjudicabitur reus ad legem suam duodecima manu.
The defendant shall be adjudged to make his law by twelve men.

343. Il covint aver' one luy xi maynz de jurer one luy, sc. que ilz entendre en lour consciens que il disoyt voier.
He must have eleven men to swear for him—that is, that they believe in their conscience that he has spoken the truth.

344. Nullus ballivus de cetero ponat aliquem ad legem manifestam, nec ad juramentum, simplici loquela sua sine testibus fidelibus ad hoc inductis.
No bailiff shall put any one to his wager of battel, or to his wager of law, on his simple declaration, without faithful witnesses brought for that purpose.

344. Si petens sectam produxerit, et concordes inveniantur, tunc reus poterit vadiare legem suam contra petentem et contra sectam suam prolatam; sed si secta variabilis inveniatur, extunc non tenebitur legem vadiare contra sectam illam.
If the plaintiff bring his witnesses, and they agree in their testimony, then the defendant may wage his law against him, and against his suit: but if the suit vary in their testimony, he will thenceforward not be bound to wage his law against that suit.

344. Ut si duos vel tres testes produxerit ad probandum, oportet quod defensio fiat per quatuor vel per sex; ita quod pro quolibet teste duos producat juratores, usque ad duodecim.
That if he bring two or three witnesses to prove the fact, the defence must be made by four or six: so that for every witness he must bring two jurors up to twelve.

350. Nisi per legale judicium parium suorum, vel per legem terræ.
Unless by the lawful judgment of his peers, or by the law of the land.

350. Nemo beneficium suum perdat, nisi secundum consuetudinem antecessorum nostrorum et per judicium pariorum suorum.

No one shall be deprived of his property, but according to the custom of our predecessors, and by the judgment of his peers.

351. De magna assisa eligenda.	Of choosing the grand assize.
351. Nisi prius.	Unless before.
351. Vexata questio.	A perplexed question.
352. Venire facias.	That you cause to come.

352. Semper dabitur dies partibus, &c. [translated in the text.]

354. Habeas corpora juratorum.	That you have the bodies of the jurors.
354. Distringas.	That you distrain.

359. Binos, trinos, vel etiam senos, ex singulis territorii quadrantibus.
Two, three, or even six, from every quarter of the country.

360. De medietate linguæ.
For having a jury consisting of half foreigners and half natives.

360. De monticolis Walliæ.	Of the mountaineers of Wales.

360. Duodeni legales homines, quorum sex Walli et sex Angli erunt, Anglis et Wallis jus dicunto.

Let twelve lawful men, of whom six shall be Welsh and six English, give their verdict for English and Welsh.

360. Jus patronatus.	A right of presentation.
361. Recusatio judicis.	Objection to the judge.

361. Propter honoris respectum; propter defectum; propter affectum; propter delictum.

On account of dignity, on account of incompetency, on account of partiality, on account of the commission of some offence.

362. Propter defectum sexus.	Because not of the male sex.
362. De ventre inspiciendo.	Of inspecting pregnancy.
363. Omni exceptione majores.	Above all exception.

363. Licebat palam excipere, et semper ex probabili causa tres repudiari: etiam plures ex causa pregnanti et manifesta.

They might openly except to, and always refuse three for a probable cause; and even more for a pregnant and manifest cause.

364. Voir dire, veritatem dicere.   To speak the truth.

---

364. Decem tales—Octo tales.   A tales of ten—A tales of eight.

---

365. Tales de circumstantibus.
A tales [such as may be wanting] from the by-standers.

---

365. Nihil sanctius, nihil antiquius fuit, perinde ac si in ipso hoc numero secreta quaedam esset religio.
Nothing was esteemed more sacred, nothing more venerable than this number, as though it contained within itself a something holy.

---

365. Fas est et ab hoste doceri.   It is right to learn even from an enemy.

---

366. Neminem voluerunt majores nostri, non modo de existimatione cujus-quam sed ne pecuniaria quidem de re minima esse judicem: nisi qui inter adversarios convenisset.
Our ancestors would have no judge concerning the reputation of a man, or even of the least pecuniary matter, but him who had been agreed upon by the contending parties.

---

366. Selecti judices.   Chosen judges.

---

366. Post urnam permittitur accusatori, ac reo, ut ex illo numero rejiciant quos putaverint sibi, aut inimicos aut ex aliqua re incommodos fore.
After the names were drawn, both the prosecutor and defendant were allowed to reject all those from the number whom they thought might from any cause be unfriendly or ill-disposed towards them.

---

366. Rejectione celebrata, in eorum locum qui rejecti fuerunt subsortie-batur praetor alios, quibus ille judicum legitimus numerus compleretur.
These being rejected, the praetor drew others to supply their place, by whom the lawful number of judges was completed.

---

366. Δικασται.   Judges.

---

366. Ei incumbit probatio, qui dicit, non qui negat; cum per rerum na-turam factum-negantis probatio nulla sit.
The proof lies on him who asserts the fact, not on him who denies it, as from the nature of things a negative is no proof.

---

368. In extremis.   In his last moments.

---

368. Instrumenta domestica, seu adnotatio, si non aliis quoque admini-culis adjuventur, ad probationem sola non sufficiunt. Nam exemplo perni-

ciosum est, ut ei scripturæ credatur, qua unusquisque sibi adnotatione propria debitorem constituit.

Private instruments, or memoranda, unless supported by other evidence, are not alone sufficient proof. For it is a dangerous precedent to give credit to any memorandum by which the writer makes another man his debtor.

369. Subpœna ad testificandum.   A subpœna to give evidence.

369. Habeas corpus ad testificandum.
That you have the body to give evidence.

369. Qui tam.   Who as well.

370. Unius responsio testis omnino non audiatur.
The evidence of one witness may never be admitted.

370. Plena probatio.   Full proof.

370. Semiplena probatio.   Half proof.

371. Nemo testis esse debet in propria causa.
No one should be a witness in his own cause.

374. Tu magis scire potes, quanta fides sit habenda testibus; qui, et cujus dignitatis, et cujus æstimationis sint; et, qui simpliciter visi sint dicere; utrum unum eundemque meditatum sermonem attulerint, an ad ea quæ interrogaveras ex tempore verisimilia responderint

You are better able to judge what faith is to be placed in witnesses; who they are, and in what credit and estimation they are held; whether they seem to speak ingenuously, and whether their answers to your questions be preconcerted, or the expressions of the moment.

376. Judicium parium.   The judgment of peers.

376. De novo.   Anew; over again.

376. In misericordia domini regis pro falso clamore suo.
At the king's mercy for his false claim.

376. Non sequitur clamorem suum. He does not pursue his claim.

378. Remittitur.   It is remitted.

383. De bene esse.
To be accepted for the present subject to future circumstances.

383. Subpœna duces tecum.   You shall take the subpœna with you.

388. Ipsi regali institutioni eleganter inserta.
Dexterously inserted in that royal institution.

---

390. Si juratores erraverint, et justiciarii secundum eorum dictum judicium pronuntiaverint, falsam faciunt pronuntiationem; et ideo sequi non debent eorum dictum, sed illud emendare tenentur per diligentem examinationem —si autem dijudicare nesciant, recurrendum erit ad majus judicium.

If the jury shall have erred, and the justices have pronounced judgment according to their verdict, they pronounce a false judgment; and therefore ought not to follow up their verdict, but are bound to amend it by a diligent examination—but if they cannot decide it, it shall be referred to a higher tribunal.

---

393. Nil debet.   He owes nothing.

---

395. Quod partes replacitent.   That the parties may replead.

---

396. Consideratum est per curiam.   It is considered by the court.

---

397. Ad executionem decretorum judicii, ad estimationem pretii, damni, lucri, &c.
To execute the decrees of court, to estimate the price, damage, gain, &c.

---

397. Non sum informatus.   I am not instructed.

---

399. Victus victori in expensis condemnandus est.
He who loses the suit pays costs to his adversary.

---

399. Eo nomine.   By that name.

---

400. Capias.   That you take.

---

400. In forma pauperis.   As a pauper.

---

404. Liberam legem.   Free law.

---

405. Si tamen evidenti, &c. [translated in the text.]

---

408. Sine calumpnia verborum, non observata illa dura consuetudine, qui cadit a syllaba, cadit a tota causa.

Without that strictness to the letter; that rigid custom not being observed, that he who fails in one syllable loses the whole cause.

---

409. Judicia perverterunt, &c. [translated in the text.]

---

410. Autres sages come leur semblera.
Such other skillful men as they shall think fit.

411. In nostra lege unum comma evertit totum placitum.
In our law one comma overturns the whole plea.

---

412. Habere facias seisinam.   That you give him seisin.

---

412. Habere facias possessionem.   That you give him possession.

---

412. De clerico admittendo.   On admitting the clerk.

---

414. Quod pœnam imprisonamenti subire non potest.
That he is not able to undergo the punishment of imprisonment.

---

415. In arcta et salva custodia.   In close and safe custody.

---

416. Cessio bonorum.   Giving up the goods.

---

416. Excommunicato capiendo.   For taking the excommunicated.

---

417. Fieri facias.   That you cause to be made.

---

417. Sed contra.   But otherwise.

---

418. De bonis ecclesiasticis.   Of ecclesiastical goods.

---

419. Elegit.   He hath chosen.

---

421. Ad infinitum.   Without restriction.

---

421. Averia carucæ.   Beasts of the plough.

---

421. Pro victu.   For the maintenance.

---

424. Dies fasti, in quibus licebat prætori fari tria verba, do, dico, addico.
Lawful days, in which the prætor was permitted the use of three
words, do, dico, addico, I give judgment, I expound the law, I execute the law.

---

427. Parens patriæ.   Parent of his country.

---

430. Hoc quidem perquam durum est, sed ita lex scripta est.
This indeed is very hard, but such is the written law.

---

431. Lex non exacte, &c. [Vide ante, vol. i., p. 62.]

---

433. Quæ in summis tribunalibus multi a legum canone decernunt judices, solus (si res exigerit) cohibet cancellarius ex arbitrio; nec aliter de-
cretis tenetur suæ curiæ vel sui ipsius, quin, elucente nova ratione, recog-
noscat quæ voluerit, mutet et deleat, prout suæ videbitur prudentiæ.

Those decisions which many judges in the highest tribunals make
according to the rules of law, the chancellor alone (if the case require it)
can restrain according to his pleasure; nor is he so bound by the decrees

of his court, or those of himself, but, a new reason appearing, he may revise whatever he pleases, may alter and reverse as he shall think fit.

436. Secundum æquum et bonum.   According to right and justice.

436. Quæ relicta sunt et tradita.   Which are left and handed down to us.

436. De jure naturæ cogitare per nos atque dicere debemus; de jure populi Romani, quæ relicta sunt et tradita.

We ought to think and decide for ourselves concerning our natural rights; but the rights of the Roman people should be determined by the laws which are left and handed down to us.

444. Pro confesso.   As acknowledged.

446. En cest court de chauncerie, home ne serra prejudice par son mispledging ou pur defaut de forme, mes solonque le veryte del mater, car il doit agarder solonque consciens, et nemi ex rigore juris.

In this court of Chancery a man shall not be prejudiced by his mispleading, or defect of form, but according to the truth of the matter; for the decision should be made according to conscience and not according to the rigor of law.

447. Dedimus potestatem.   We have given the power.

452. Nota est sponsio judicialis: "Spondesne quingentos, si meus sit? Spondeo, si tuus sit. Et tu quoque spondesne quingentos, ni tuus sit? Spondeo, ni meus sit."

The judicial wager is known: "Do you engage to give me five hundred pounds, if it be mine? I promise it, if it be thine. And you also, Do you promise me five hundred pounds if it be not thine? I promise it, if it be not mine.

453. Caveat.   That he take care.

NOTE AT THE END OF WILLIAM'S EDITION.

499. Catalla felonum.   The goods of felons.

500. Descriptio Normanniæ hujusque Normanniæ consuetudinis latorem sive datorem, Sanctum Edwardum Angliæ regem, &c.

A description of Normandy and its custom, by the lawgiver, Edward the Confessor, King of England, &c.

500. Ad probandum aliquid per credentiam duodecim hominum vicinorum.

To prove a circumstance by the testimony of twelve men of the vicinage.

500. A posse ad esse non valet argumentum.

No argument of the actual existence of a thing, from the possibility of its existence avails.

A

TRANSLATION,

&c., &c.

VOLUME THE FOURTH.

8. MALA prohibita.   Crimes because forbidden.

8. Mala in se.   Crimes in themselves.

9. Non igitur magis est contra naturam morbus aut egestas aut quid hujusmodi quam detractio aut appetitio alieni.

Therefore, neither disease, indigence, nor any evil of the same kind is more contrary to nature than the appropriating, or desiring to appropriate, the property of another to our own use.

11. Ut pœna ad paucos, metus ad omnes perveniat.
That few may suffer, but all may dread punishment.

16. Ea sunt animadvertenda peccata maxime, quæ difficillime præcaventur.
Those offences should be most severely punished, which it is most difficult to guard against.

17. De bigamis.   Of those guilty of bigamy.

17. Ultimum supplicium.   The severest or capital punishment.

21. In foro conscientiæ.   At the tribunal of conscience.

22. Infantia.   Infancy.

22. Pueritia.   Childhood.

22. Ætas infantiæ proxima.   The age nearest infancy.

22. Ætas pubertati proxima.   The age nearest puberty.

23. Malitia supplet aetatem.   Malice is held equivalent to age.

___

23. Doli incapax.   Incapable of guile.

___

23. Doli capax.   Capable of guile.

___

23. Prima facie.   Immediately—At first sight.

___

24. Furiosus furore solum punitur.
A madman is punished by his madness alone.

___

25. Compos mentis.   Of sane mind.

___

26. Voluntarius dæmon.   A voluntary madman.

___

26. Nam omne crimen ebrietas, et incendit et detegit.
For drunkenness excites to and discloses every crime.

___

26. Per vinum delapsis capitalis poena remittitur.
Capital punishment is remitted, where the crime has been occasioned
by ebriety.

___

29. Procul dubio quod alterum libertas, alterum necessitas impelleret.
Because doubtless the one did it of his own free will, the other of
necessity.

___

30. Pro timore mortis, et recesserunt quam cito potuerunt.
Through fear of death, and quitted on the first opportunity.

___

30. Qui cadere possit in virum constantem, non timidum et meticulosum.
As might seize a courageous man not timid or fearful.

___

31. Suum cuique incommodum ferendum est, potius quam de alterius
commodis detrahendum.
Every one must bear his own inconvenience, rather than detract
from the convenience of another.

___

36. Propter odium delicti. On account of the heinousness of the offence.

___

36. Quæ de minimis non curat.
Does not take cognizance of slight matters.

___

36. Accessorius sequitur naturam sui principalis.
The accessory follows the condition of his principal.

___

37. In rerum natura.   In the nature of things—Born.

___

37. Ex post facto.   After the fact.

___

38. Unum qui consilium daret, alterum qui contractaret, tertium qui re-
ceptaret et occuleret; pari poenæ singulos obnoxios.

He who should plan a robbery, he who should commit it, and thirdly, he who should receive and conceal the stolen goods; each liable to an equal degree of punishment.

44. Utiles esse opiniones has, quis negat, cum intelligat, quam multa firmentur jurejurando; quantæ salutis sint fœderum religiones; quam multos divini supplicii metus a scelere revocarit; quamque sancta sit societas civium inter ipsos, Diis immortalibus interpositis tum judicibus, tum testibus.

Who can deny that these opinions are useful when he sees how many things are confirmed by oath; what security religion gives to compacts; how many are reclaimed from wickedness by the fear of divine punishment; and how sacred and inviolate is the bond of society between citizens, the presence of the immortal gods being impressed on the minds, as well of the judges, as of the witnesses?

44. Pro salute animæ.   For the health of the soul.

45. Sententia rerum divinarum humano sensu excogitata, palam docta et pertinaciter defensa.

Doctrines, in religion, of human invention, openly taught and pertinaciously defended.

45. Hæreticus est qui dubitat de fide Catholica, et qui negligit servare ea, quæ Romana ecclesia statuit, seu servare decreverat.

A heretic is one who doubts concerning the Catholic faith, and who neglects to observe those things which the Roman church has appointed, or ordained.

45. In pios usus.   To pious uses.

45. Ut citra mortis periculum sententia circa eum moderatur.

That the sentence with respect to him might be mitigated so as not to involve him in the danger of losing his life.

46. De hæretico comburendo.   For burning a heretic.

47. Ex officio.   By virtue of his office — officially.

47. Non compos mentis.   Of unsound mind.

53. Mandamus.   We command.

59. Scripture est common ley, sur quel touts manieres de leis sont fondes.

The Scriptures are the common law on which every kind of law is founded.

65. Custos morum.   Preserver of the manners.

65. Contra bonos mores.   Against good manners.

71. Hostis humani generis.   An enemy to mankind.

75. Crimen læse majestatis.   The crime of læse-majesty. [High-treason.]

76. A vinculo matrimonii.   From the bond of matrimony.

76. A mensa et thoro.   From bed and board.

76. Qui de nece virorum illustrium, qui consiliis et consistorio nostro intersunt, senatorum etiam (nam et ipsi pars corporis nostri sunt) vel cujuslibet postremo, qui militat nobiscum cogitaverit: (eadem enim severitate voluntatem sceleris, qua effectum puniri jura voluerint) ipse quidem, utpote majestatis reus, gladio feriatur, bonis ejus omnibus fisco nostro addictis.

Ie who shall meditate the death of any of those illustrious men who assist at our councils; likewise of the senators (for they are a part of ourself) or lastly of any of our companions in arms; shall, forasmuch as he is guilty of treason, perish by the sword, and all his goods be confiscated: for the law will punish the intention, and the perpetration of the crime with equal severity.

76. Lex Julia majestatis.   The Julian law concerning treason.

77. De facto.   In fact.

77. De jure.   By right.

78. Per infortunium.   By mischance.

79. Voluntas pro facto.   The will for the deed.

80. Scribere est agere.   To write is to act.

86. Casus omissi.   Cases unsettled.

88. Custos rotulorum.   Keeper of the Rolls.

88. De falsa moneta.   Of false money.

89. De moneta.   Of money.

90   Aliudve quid simile si admiserint.
       Or if they committed anything of the same kind.

92. Jure divino.   By divine right.

92. Vox populi vox Dei.   The voice of the people is the voice of God.

95. Fallo, fefelli.   To deceive.

95. Crimen animo felleo perpetratum.
     A crime perpetrated with a bitter inclination.

96. Scilicet, per quas feudum amittitur.   That is, by which the fee is lost.

96. Si domino deservire, &c. [Vide ante, vol. ii., p. 284.]

96. Si dominum cucurbitaverit, i. e. cum uxore ejus concubuerit.
     If he dishonor his lord, that is, lie with his wife.

96. Si fecerit feloniam, dominum forte cucurbitando.
     If he commit felony, as by dishonoring his lord.

97. Per laudamentum sive judicium parium.
     By the verdict or judgment of his peers.

106. [Homines] A latere.   Attendants on a prince.

107. Beneficia.   Benefices.

107. Etiamsi ad illa personæ consueverint et debuerint per electionem
aut quemvis alium modum assumi.

     Although parsons were accustomed, and ought, to be admitted to
them by election, or some other manner.

114. Execrabile illud statutum.   That execrable statute.

115. Passim.   Everywhere—In many places.

115. Imperium in imperio.   A government within a government.

118. Præmunire—To forewarn. [Vide Commentaries, vol. iv., p. 103.]

121. Voluntas regis in curia, non in camera.
     The will of the king in his court, not in his chamber.

124. Quibus major reverentia et securitas debetur; ut templa et judicia,
quæ sancta habebantur—arces et aulæ regis—denique locus quilibet præ-
sente aut adventante rege.

     To which a greater reverence and inviolability is due; as churches
and courts of justice, which were held sacred—the king's courts and castles
—lastly, the place where the king resides or to which he is approaching.

127. Paterfamilias.   The father of a family.

127. De medietate. A jury, one half natives, the other half foreigners.

129. Inter alia.   Among other things.
                    8

130. De frangentibus prisonam.   Concerning those breaking prison.

134. Latroni cum similem habuit, qui furtum celare vellet, et occulte sine judice compositionem ejus admittere.

Considers him, who would conceal a theft, and secretly receive a composition for it without the knowledge of the judge, in the same light as the thief.

135. Qui improbe cœunt in alienam litem, ut quicquid ex condemnatione in rem ipsius redactum fuerit inter eos communicaretur, lege Julia de vi privata tenentur.

Those who knavishly interfere in other men's suits, for the purpose of sharing whatever may be awarded by the verdict, are liable to the Julian law de vi privata [of secret influence.]

136. Liberam legem.   Free law — Legal rights.

137. Malo animo.   With an evil intention.

137. Crimen falsi.   Forgery.

139. Perjurii pœna divina, exitium ; humana, dedecus.

The divine punishment of perjury is death; the human punishment, disgrace.

146. Ab ingressu ecclesiæ.   From entering the church.

147. Posse comitatus.   The power of the county.

149. Habent legibus sanctum, si quis de republica a finitimis rumore aut fama acceperit, uti ad magistratum deferat, neve cum alio communicet, quod sæpe homines temerarios atque imperitos falsis rumoribus terreri, et ad facinus impelli, et de summis rebus consilium capere cognitum est.

They make it an inviolable rule, that if any one shall have received any intelligence in the neighborhood concerning the republic by rumor or report, he shall make it known to a magistrate, and not communicate it to any one else: for rash and ignorant men, it is well known, alarmed by false reports, are often driven to violent measures, and interfere in affairs of the highest consequence.

150. Asperis facetiis inlusus, quæ ubi multum ex vero traxere, acrem sui memoriam relinquunt.

Being rallied with cutting jests, which, when they contain much truth, leave a bitter remembrance behind.

151. Ex ratione officii.   From the design of the office.

151.   ————Quinetiam lex
        Pœnaque lata, malo quæ nollet carmine quenquam
        Describi:— vertere modum formidine fustis.

Moreover the law and punishment are decreed, which forbids any one to write scurrilous verses:—they changed their mode of writing through fear of corporal chastisement.

155. Instar omnium.	Equal to them all.
157. Ipso facto.	By that fact.
157. Post obit.	After he dies.
157. Christiani Judaizantes.	Judaizing Christians.

157. Cum ille, qui quæsierat, dixisset, Quid fœnerari? Tum Cato, quid hominem, inquit, occidere.

When the interrogator asked, What could be compared with lending on usury? Cato answered, Any thing which can kill a man.

157. Malam cerevisiam faciens, in cathedra ponebatur stercoris.

He who made bad beer, was placed in a dung-cart.

158. Ab initio.	From the beginning.
158. Qui tam.	Who as well.

159. Pœna viginti aureorum statuitur adversus eum, qui contra annonam fecerit, societatemve coierit, quo annona carior fiat.

Those who entered into any association, or employed any other means, by which the price of provisions was enhanced, were amerced in a fine of twenty guineas.

164. Prope soli barbarorum singulis uxoribus contenti sunt.

Almost the only barbarians who are contented with one wife.

164. Omni privilegio clericali nudati, et coercioni fori secularis addicti.

They were stripped of every clerical privilege, and given up to the power of the secular court.

168. Rixatrix, calumniatrix, communis pugnatrix, communis pacis perturbatrix.

A scold, a slanderer, a common brawler, a common disturber of the peace.

174. Contra bonos mores.	Against good manners.

177. Pars muletæ regi, vel civitati, pars ipsi, qui vindicatur vel propinquis ejus, exsolvitur.

Part of the fine is paid to the king or the state, and part to the plaintiff, or to his relations.

178. Istud homicidium, si fit ex livore, vel delectatione effundendi

humanum sanguinem, licet juste occidatur iste, tamen occisor peccat mortaliter, propter intentionem corruptam.

If the homicide be committed through malice, or a thirst of human blood, the perpetrator is guilty of murder on account of his evil intention, although the sufferer deserved death.

179. Servato juris ordine.   According to the order of the court.

180. Furem, si aliter capi non posset, occidere permittunt.
It is allowable to kill a thief if he cannot otherwise be taken.

180. De malefactoribus in parcis.   Of trespassers in parks.

181. Divus Hadrianus, &c. [translated in the text.]

183. Immoderate suo jure utatur, tunc reus homicidii sit.
He use his right beyond the bounds of moderation, then he is guilty of homicide.

185. Vindices injuriarum.   Avengers of injuries.

185. Qui cum aliter tueri se non possunt, damni culpam dederint, innoxii sunt.
Those, who when they cannot otherwise defend themselves, kill their adversary, are held innocent.

186. A fortiori.   By a stronger reason.

187. Necessitas culpabilis.   Culpable necessity.

187. Annotatione principis.   With the signature of the prince.

188. Νήπιος ουχ εδελων.   Careless but unintentional.

189. Si quis impatientia doloris, aut taedio vitæ, aut morbo, aut furore, aut pudore, mori maluit, non aniamadvertatur in eum.
If any one, sinking under the pressure of grief, or weariness of life, disease, madness, or shame, shall prefer death, his conduct shall not be considered to the prejudice of his character.

191. Homicidia vulgaria; quæ aut casu aut etiam sponte committuntur, sed in subitaneo quodam iracundiæ calore et impetu.
Common homicides, which are committed by accident, or even willingly, but in the sudden heat and violence of passion.

191. Furor brevis.   Short madness.

194. Nos, divini juris rigorem moderantes, &c.
We, mitigating the rigor of divine law, &c.

195. Je riens ne celerai, ne sufferai estre cele ne murdre.

Nullum veritatem celabo, nec celari permittam nec murdrari.

I will not hide the truth, nor will I permit it to be hidden or concealed.

195. Pur murdre le droit.

Pro jure alicujus murdriendo.

For concealing the right of any one.

195. Homicidium quod nullo vidente, nullo sciente, clam perpetratur.

Homicide, which is committed privately, no one witnessing, no one knowing it.

196. Peculiari pœna judicem puniunt; peculiari testes, quorum fides judicem seduxit; peculiari denique et maxima auctorem, ut homicidam.

There is one particular punishment inflicted on the judge, another on the witnesses whose testimony misled the judge; and lastly, one, of the greatest severity, on the prosecutor, who is treated as a murderer.

197. Lex Cornelia de sicariis.   The Cornelian law concerning assassins.

198. Un disposition a faire un male chose.

A disposition to commit a bad action.

200. Eundo, morando et redeundo. In going, remaining, and returning.

202. Famosos latrones, in his locis, ubi grassati sunt, furca figendos placuit; ut, et conspectu deterreantur alii, et solatio sit cognatis interemptorum eodem loco pœna reddita, in quo latrones homicidia fecissent.

Notorious robbers were fastened to a gibbet in the places where they had committed the act: that others might be deterred by the sight, and also that the relations of the deceased might be comforted with the knowledge that punishment was inflicted on the very spot where the murder had been done.

203. Omnium gravissima censetur vis facta ab incolis in patriam, subditis in regem, liberis in parentes, maritis in uxores (et vice versa), servis in dominos, aut etiam ab homine in semetipsum.

That violence which is exerted by inhabitants against their country, by subjects against their king, by children against their parents, by husbands against their wives, by wives against their husbands, by servants against their masters, or even by man against himself, is considered as the worst of all crimes.

206. Membrum pro membro.   Limb for limb.

206. Mes, si la pleynte soit faite de femme qu'avera tolle a home ses membres, en tiel case perdra le feme la une meyn par jugement, come le membre dount ele avera trespasse.

But if the complaint be preferred against a woman that she had mutilated a man, she shall be adjudged to lose her hand, as the member with which she had offended.

---

206. Et sequitur aliquando pœna capitalis, aliquando perpetuum exilium, cum omnium bonorum ademptione.

..And sometimes capital punishment follows, sometimes perpetual exile with the loss of all his goods.

---

210. Sive volentibus, sive nolentibus mulieribus, tale facinus fuerit perpetratum.

The crime will be the same whether the woman consent or not.

---

210. Si enim ipsi raptores metu, vel atrocitate pœnæ, ab hujusmodi facinore se temperaverint, nulli mulieri, sive volenti, sive nolenti, peccandi locus relinquetur: quia hoc ipsum velle mulierum, ab insidiis nequissimi hominis, qui meditatur rapinam, inducitur. Nisi etenim eam solicitaverit, nisi odiosis artibus circumvenerit, non faciet eam velle in tantum dedecus sese prodere.

For if the ravisher be restrained from a crime of this nature, either through fear, or the severity of the punishment, no opportunity is left for a woman to offend either willingly or unwillingly, because the desire is always raised in her by the wicked seductions of the man who meditates the violence. For unless he solicit her, unless he compass his design by odious arts, he could never make her wish to betray herself to such dishonor.

---

211. Dum recens fuerit maleficium. While the injury be recent.

---

211. Nullum tempus occurrit regi. No time runs against the king.

---

213. Licet meretrix fuerit antea, certe tunc temporis non fuit, cum reclamando nequitiæ ejus consentire noluit.

Although she had been a harlot formerly, she surely was not at that time, when by crying out she showed herself unwilling to consent to his wickedness.

---

213. Salvo pudore.   Decency being observed.

---

215. Peccatum illud horribile, inter Christianos non nominandum.

That horrible crime not to be named among Christians.

---

215. Ubi scelus est id, quod non proficit scire, jubemus insurgere leges, armari jura gladio ultore, ut exquisitis pœnis subdantur infames, qui sunt, vel qui futuri sunt rei.

Where that crime is found, which it is unfit even to know, we command the law to arise armed with an avenging sword, that the infamous men who are, or shall in future be guilty of it, may undergo the most severe punishments.

---

216. Agentes et consentientes pari pœna plectantur.

The perpetrator and consenting party are both liable to the same punishment.

- 217. Articuli cleri.   Articles of the clergy.

---

217. Pro correctione et salute animæ.
For the amendment and health of his soul.

---

220. Ab ardendo.   From burning.

---

221. Voluntas reputatur pro facto.   The will is taken for the deed.

---

221. Quando aliquid prohibetur, prohibetur et omne, per quod devenitur ad illud.

When any thing is prohibited, every thing which may lead to it is prohibited also.

---

222. Incendit et combussit.   He hath burned and consumed.

---

222. Eos, qui negligenter ignes apud se habuerint, fustibus vel flagellis cædi.

Those who have fire carelessly about them shall be beaten with whips or sticks.

---

223. Quid enim sanctius, quid omni religione munitius, quam domus uniuscujusque civium?

For what is more sacred, what more inviolable, than the house of every citizen?

---

224. Crepusculum.   Twilight.

---

224. Domus mansionalis Dei.   The mansion house of God.

---

225. Nocturna diruptio alicujus habitaculi, vel ecclesiæ, etiam murorum portarumve burgi, ad feloniam perpetrandam.

The nocturnal breaking open of any habitation or church, or even the walls or gates of a town, for the purpose of committing a felony.

---

225. Animo revertendi.   With the intention of returning.

---

226. Clausum fregit.   Breaking the close.

---

230. Meum et tuum.   Mine and thine.

---

230. Animo furandi.   With an intention of stealing.

---

232. Lucri causa.   For the sake of gain.

---

235. Feræ naturæ.   Of a wild nature.

236. Domitæ naturæ.

Of a tame nature.

236. Invito domino.

Against the will of the owner.

236. Lex Hostilia de furtis.

The Hostilian law concerning theft.

237. Est enim ad vindicanda furta nimis atrox, nec tamen ad refrænanda sufficiens; quippe neque furtum simplex tam ingens facinus est, ut capite debeat plecti; neque ulla pœna est tanta, ut ab latrociniis cohibeat eos, qui nullam aliam artem quærendi victus habent.—Denique, cum lex Mosaica, quanquam inclemens et aspera; tamen pecunia furtum, haud morte, mulctavit; ne putemus Deum, in nova lege clementiæ qua pater imperat filiis, majorem indusisse nobis invicem sæviendi licentiam. Hæc sunt cur non licere putem; quam vero sit absurdum, atque etiam perniciosum reipublicæ, furem atque homicidam ex æquo puniri, nemo est (opinor) qui nesciat.

Death is too severe a punishment for theft, nor yet sufficient to restrain it; for neither is simple theft such a heinous offence, that it should be made capital, nor can there be any punishment so severe as to restrain those from robbing who have no other means of obtaining a livelihood.— In short, since the Mosaic law, although rigorous and severe, only punished theft by a fine, not by death, we cannot think that God, in that new law or mercy by which as a father he governs his children, has granted us a greater liberty of harshness or severity towards each other. These are the reasons why I deem it unlawful. And there is no one, I think, but must be sensible how absurd it is, and even pernicious to the commonwealth, that a thief and murderer should receive the same punishment.

239. Solidus legalis.

Lawful shilling.

240. Onus probandi.

The burden of proof.

243. Qui vi rapuit, fur improbior esse videtur.
He who hath taken by force, seems to be the more iniquitous thief.

252. Tradat fidejussores de pace et legalitate tuenda.
Let him deliver sureties for maintaining peace and good behavior.

253. Ex officio.

Officially.

253. Supplicavit.

He hath supplicated.

256. Contra pacem.

Against the peace.

259. Pro re nata.

For present emergency.

260. Licet apud consilium accusare quoque, et discrimen capitis intendere.
It is allowed to bring accusations before the council, and to commence capital prosecutions.

261. Dum bene se gesserit.
While he shall have conducted himself well.

---

261. Pro hac vice.   For the special case.

---

262. Quand un seigneur de parlement serra arrein de treason ou felony, le roy par ses lettres patents fera un grand et sage seigneur d'estre le grand seneschal d'Angleterre: qui doit faire un precept pur faire venir xx seigneurs ou xviii, &c.

When a lord of parliament is arraigned on a charge of treason or felony, the king by his letters patent shall create some wise and noble peer Lord High Steward of England, who shall issue out a precept to summon eighteen or twenty lords, &c.

---

262. Secundum legem et consuetudinem Angliæ.
According to the law and custom of England.

---

262. Certiorari.   To have notice given him.

---

263. Pro tempore.   For the time.

---

264. Expiscopi, sicut cæteri barones, debent interesse judiciis cum baronibus, quousque perveniatur ad diminutionem membrorum, vel ad mortem.

The bishops ought to be present at trials, as well as the other barons, unless they involve the loss of life or limb.

---

265. Durante viduitate.   During widowhood.

---

265. Nisi prius.   Unless before.

---

266. Jure vetusto obtinuit, quievisse omnia inferiora judicia, dicente jus rege.

It was the ancient practice that all inferior courts of justice should be discontinued in those places where the king administered justice.

---

266. Oyer et terminer.   To hear and determine.

---

266. En la chaumbre des esteiles pres la resceipt la Westminster.
In the star chamber near the Exchequer at Westminster.

---

266. De computatione procuratorum. Of the stewards' accounts.

---

266. In fine computi fiat starrum per modum dividendæ, in quo ponentur omnia remanentia in communi cista tam pignora quam pecunia, ac etiam arreragia et debita, ita quod omnibus constare poterit evidenter, in quo statu tunc universitas fuerit quoad bona, &c.

Finally he shall cause an inventory to be made under distinct heads, in which all that remains in the common chest, as well securities as money,

and also arrears and debts, shall be inserted, that it may be evident to all
in what state the university be, as to its effects, &c.

270. De bono et malo.   Of good and evil.

272. Custos rotulorum.   Keeper of the Rolls.

274. De omnibus quidem cognoscit, non tamen de omnibus judicat.
Takes cognizance of all offences, but does not give judgment in all.

274. Levari facias.   That you cause to be levied.

274. Super visum corporis.   On view of the body.

278. Ad inquirendum.   To inquire.

278. Ad audiendum et determinandum.   To hear and determine.

278. Inter minora crimina.   Among the lesser crimes.

278. Laicos privilegio universitatis gaudentes.
Laymen enjoying the privilege of the university.

283.   Qui statuit aliquid, parte inaudita altera,
              Æquum licet statuerit, haud æquus fuit.

He who prefers a charge against another, however just it may be,
will himself be unjust, unless the accused be heard in his own defence.

284. Supersedeas.
A command to stay or forbear doing that which ought not to be done.

286. A qua non deliberentur sine speciali præcepto domini regis.
From which they may not be released without special command of
the king.

288. In personam.   Against the person.

288. In rem.   Against the matter or thing.

292. A fortiori.   By a stronger reason.

292. Virtute officii.   By virtue of their office.

293. De officio coronatoris.   Of the office of coroner.

296. Nemo tenebatur prodere seipsum.
No one was obliged to betray himself.

298. In omnibus placitis de felonia solet accusatus per plegios dimitti, præterquam in placito de homicidio, ubi ad terrorem aliter statutum est.

In all pleas of felony the accused is usually discharged upon bail, except in the plea of murder, where, to deter others, it is otherwise decreed.

299. De excommunicato capiendo.

For taking an excommunicated person.

299. In omnibus placitis de felonia solet accusatus per plegios dimitti, præterquam in placito de homicidio.—Sciendum tamen quod, in hoc placito, non solet accusatus per plegios dimitti, nisi ex regiæ potestatis beneficio.

In all pleas of felony the accused is usually discharged upon bail, except in the plea of murder.—Nevertheless it should be observed that, in this plea, it is not customary to discharge the accused on bail, unless through favor of the royal authority.

300. Mittimus. We send or commit.

300. Custodes pœnam sibi commissorum non augeant, nec eos torqueant; sed omni sævitia remota, pietateque adhibita, judicia debite exequantur.

Let not gaolers torture or augment the punishment of those entrusted to their keeping; but let the sentence of the law be duly yet mercifully executed.

302. Exeant seniores duodecim thani, et præfectus cum eis, et jurent super sanctuarium quod eis in manus datur, quod nolint ullum innocentem accusare, nec aliquem noxium celare.

Let twelve elder freemen, and the foreman with them, retire and swear upon the holy book which is given into their hands that they will not accuse any innocent person, nor screen any criminal.

307. In manu. In his hand.

307. Flagrante delicto. In open crime.

309. Certiorari. To have notice given him.

310. Custos morum. Keeper of the morals.

312. Quo warranto. By what warrant.

313. Luitur homicidium certo armentorum ac pecorum numero; recipitque satisfactionem universa domus.

The whole family receives satisfaction, and the homicide is expiated by a certain recompense in flocks and herds.

313. Delictis, pro modo pœnarum, equorum pecorumque numero convicti mulctantur. Pars mulctæ regi vel civitati; pars ipsi qui vindicatur, vel propinquis ejus, exsolvitur.

Those who are convicted of offences are punished by a fine of a certain number of horses and cattle. One part of the fine is paid to the king or state, the other part to the plaintiff or his relations.

315. Præscriptio annalis, quæ currit adversus actorem; si de homicida ei non constet intra annum a cæde facta, nec quenquam interea arguat et accuset.

The limitation of a year, which runs against the appellor, if he prove not the homicide within a year from its perpetration, or bring his accusation within that time.

315. Nemo bis punitur pro eodem delicto.
No one is punished twice for the same offence.

316. Nam quilibet potest renunciare juri pro se introducto.
For any one may relinquish a right introduced for his own avail.

318. Venire facias.   That you cause to come.

319. Quinto exactus.   Required the fifth time.

319. Exigi facias.   That you cause to be required.

320. Caput lupinum.   A wolf's head.

320. Capias utlagatum.   That you take the outlaw.

323. Constat de persona.   There is evidence of the person.

323. Non constitit.   It was not evident.

324. Ex visitatione Dei.   By the visitation of God.

325. Forte et dure.   Strong and hard.

325. Trina admonitio.   A third warning.

326. De inope debitore secando. " Eo consilio tanta immanitas pœnæ denunciata est, ne ad eam unquam perveniretur."
Of cutting the insolvent debtor into pieces. "Such a cruelty of punishment was denounced in that law, that it never was put in execution."

326. Dissectum esse antiquitus neminem equidem neque legi neque audivi.
I have neither read nor heard that anciently any debtor was ever cut into pieces.

327. Tamen illa tormenta gubernat dolor, moderatur natura cujusque tum animi tum corporis, regit quæsitor, flectit libido, corrumpit spes, infirmat metus, ut in tot rerum angustiis nihil veritati loci relinquatur.

Nevertheless, these torments are regulated by pain; they are more or less great in each sufferer, according to his strength of mind or body, the inquisitor directs them, the will bends, hope corrupts, fear enfeebles, so that in the dread and distraction of his situation, there is no place left for the consideration of truth.

---

327. Al common ley, &c. [translated in the text.]

---

328. Et fuit dit, que le contraire avoit estre fait devant ces heures.
And it was said, that the contrary had been done before this time.

---

330. Ex debito justitiæ.   As due to justice.

---

336. Cessante ratione, cessat et ipsa lex.
The reason ceasing, the law itself ceases.

---

338. Nil debet.   He owes nothing.

---

338. Quia interest reipublicæ ut sit finis litium.
Because it is for the public good that there be an end to contentions.

---

338. In favorem vitæ.   From a regard to life.

---

339. Proditorie et contra ligeantie suæ debitum.
Traitorously and against his due allegiance.

---

339. Felonice.   Feloniously.

---

341. Non inde est culpabilis, et pro bono et malo ponit se super patriam.
He is not guilty of this, and for good and for ill puts himself on his country.

---

341. Ponit se super patriam.   He puts himself upon his country.

---

341. Ore tenus.   By word of mouth.

---

341. Pro confesso.   As confessed.

---

341. Judicium Dei.   The judgment of God.

---

342. Vulgaris purgatio.   Common purgation.

---

343. Tenetur se purgare is qui accusatur, per Dei judicium; scilicet per calidum ferrum, vel per aquam, pro diversitate conditionis hominum : per ferrum calidum si fuerit homo liber; per aquam si fuerit rusticus.
The accused party is bound to clear himself by the judgment of God; that is, either by hot iron, or by water, according to his rank: by hot iron, if he be a free-man; by water, if of inferior degree.

344. Judicium ferri, aquæ et ignis.   The judgment of iron, water, and fire.

344. Non defuit illis operæ et laboris pretium; semper enim ab ejusmodi judicio aliquid lucri sacerdotibus obveniebat.

They did not go without reward for their pains and labor; for from judgments of this kind some gain always accrued to the priests.

344. Cum sit contra præceptum Domini, non tentabis Dominum Deum tuum.

Since it is against the commandment of the Lord—thou shalt not tempt the Lord thy God.

345. Per buccellam deglutiendam abjuravit.

He abjured it by swallowing the morsel of execration.

349. Nullus liber homo, &c. [Vide ante, vol. ii., p. 93.]

350. Palladium.   A safeguard—A wooden image of Pallas.

351. Certiorari.   To have notice given him.

351. Nolle prosequi.   Will not prosecute.

351. Quo warranto.   By what warrant.

352. Omni exceptione majores.   Above all exception.

352. Propter honoris respectum, &c. [Vide ante, vol. iii., p. 361.]

353. In favorem vitæ.   From a regard to life.

355. Instanter.   Instantly.

355. De causis criminalibus vel capitalibus nemo quærat consilium; quin implacitatus statim perneget, sine omni petitione consilii. In aliis omnibus potest et debet uti consilio.

In criminal or capital cases let no man crave imparlance; but without pleading, and without craving leave to imparl, let him immediately and positively deny. In all other cases he can and ought to have imparlance.

355. Apres ce, est tend le querelle a respondre; et aura congie de soy conseiller, s'il le demande; et quand il sera conseille, il peut nyer le faict dont ill est accuse.

Querelatus autem postea tenetur respondere; et habebit licentiam consulendi, si requirat; habito autem consilio, debet factum negare quo accusatus est.

But the defendant is afterwards bound to answer; and he shall have the liberty of imparling if he require it; but imparlance being had, he ought to deny the fact of which he is accused.

360. Scintilla juris.   A spark of law.

363. Spoliatus debet, ante omnia, restitui.
Restitution should be made to the person robbed, before all others.

366. Jure divino.   By divine right.

367. Habitum et tonsuram clericalem.   The clerical habit and tonsure.

367. Miserere mei Deus.   Have mercy on me, O God.

369. Absque purgatione facienda.   Without making purgation.

371. Privilegium clericale.   The clerical privilege—Benefit of clergy.

372. De clero.   Of clergy.

372. Denarii.   Pence.

379. Liber homo non amercietur pro parvo delicto, nisi secundum modum
ipsius delicti; et pro magno delicto, secundum magnitudinem delicti;
salvo contenemento suo; et mercator eodem modo, salva mercandisa sua;
et villanus eodem modo amercietur, salvo wainagio suo.

A free man shall be amerced for a small offence, only according to its
measure; and for a great offence, only according to its magnitude, saving
his land; and the merchant in the same manner, saving his merchandize;
and a villain shall be amerced in the same manner, saving his wainage.

370. Sit in misericordia.   Let him be at the mercy.

380. Quantum inde regi dare valeat per annum, salva sustentatione sua,
et uxoris, et liberorum suorum.

How much he could pay a year to the king, saving his maintenance,
and the maintenance of his wife and children.

380. Qui non habet in crumena luat in corpore.
Let him, who has nothing in purse, pay in person.

382. Nec vero me fugit quam sit acerbum, parentum scelera filiorum
poenis lui: sed hoc praeclare legibus comparatum est, ut caritas liberorum
amiciores parentes reipublicæ redderet.

Nor has it escaped me how hard it is, that the crimes of parents
should be atoned for by the punishment of their sons; but it is wisely
provided by the laws, that affection for their children may make parents
more faithful to the republic.

383. Ibi esse poenam, ubi et noxa est.
That where the crime is there the punishment should be.

383. Peccata suos teneant auctores, nec ulterius progrediatur metus, quam
reperiatur delictum

Crimes should affect only the perpetrators of them, and the dread of punishment not extend beyond the sphere of offence.

385. De prerogativo regis.	Of the king's prerogative.
385. Ex gratia.	As matter of favor.
385. Ex arbitrio judicis.	At the will of the judge.
388. Ex parte materna.	By the mother's side.
394. Ex necessitate legis.	From legal necessity.
395. In favorem prolis.	In favor of the offspring.

395. Quod prægnantis mulieris damnatæ pœna differatur, quoad pariat.
That the punishment of a pregnant woman condemned, shall be deferred till after her delivery.

396. Furiosus solo furore punitur.
A madman is punished by his madness alone.

397. A lege suæ dignitatis.	From the law of his dignity.

398. Non potest rex gratiam facere cum injuria et damno aliorum.
The king cannot confer a favor by the injury and loss of others.

400. Item prie la commune a nostre dit seigneur le roi que nul pardon soit grante a nully persone, petit ne grande, q'ont este de son counseil et serementez, et sont empeschez en cest present parlement de vie ne de membre, fyn ne de raunceon, de forfaiture des terres, tennemenz, biens, ou chateux, lesqueux sont ou serront trovez en aucun defaut encontre leur ligeance, et la tenure de leur dit serement: mais q'ils ne serront jammes conseillers ne officers du roi, mais en tout oustez de la courte de roi et de conseil as touz jours. Et sur ceo soit en present parlement fait estatut s'il plest au roi, et de touz autres en temps a venir en cas semblables, pur profit du roi et du roialme.

Responsio.—Le roi ent fra sa volente, come mieltz lui semblera.

Also the commons pray our said lord the king, that no pardon be granted to any persons, high or low, who have been sworn of his council, and are impeached in this present parliament of life and limb; and not to release those who are or shall be found to fail in their allegiance and the tenure of their said oath, from forfeiture of their lands, tenements, goods or chattels; that they shall never be councillors or officers of the king, but be forever excluded from his court and council. And for this purpose may it please the king that an act be passed in this present parliament, and all others, in time to come in like cases, for the profit of the king and realm.

Answer.—The king will do his pleasure in this matter, as it shall seem best to him.

| 401. Non obstante. | Notwithstanding. |

| 402. Pro defectu hæredis. | For want of an heir. |

405. Judicandum est legibus, non exemplis.
We must judge by the laws, not by examples.

| 411. Liber judicialis. | Judgment book. |

| 412. Commune consilium. | The common council. |

| 421. Congé d'eslire. | Leave to elect. |

424. Nullus liber homo capiatur vel imprisonetur, aut disscisiatur de libero tenemento suo vel libertatibus vel liberis consuetudinibus suis, aut utlagetur, aut exulet, aut aliquo modo destruatur, nec super eum ibimus, nec super eum mittemus, nisi per legale judicium parium suorum vel per legem terræ. Nulli vendemus, nulli negabimus, aut differemus rectum vel judicium.

No free man may be taken, or imprisoned, or disseised of his freehold, liberties, or free customs, or be outlawed, or exiled, or in any manner deprived of life, nor will we go or send against him, but by the lawful judgment of his peers or by the law of the land. To none will we sell, to none deny, to none delay either right or justice.

424. Charta libertatum regni. The charter of the liberties of the kingdom.

| 425. Liberi homines. | Free men. |

425. Ad concordiam publicam promovendam.
For promoting the public peace.

425. Per commune concilium et assensum omnium episcoporum, et principum, comitum; et omnium sapientum seniorum, et populorum totius regni.
By the common council and assent of all the bishops, princes, earls, wise men and elders, and the commons of the whole kingdom.

425. Per commune cansilium et assensum omnium episcoporum, procerum, comitum, et sapientum, seniorum, et populorum, et per preceptum regis Inæ.
By the common council and assent of all the bishops, peers, earls, wise men, and elders, and the people, and by the command of King Ina.

428. Nam silent leges inter arma. For laws are silent midst the din of arms.

| 439. De odio et atia. | Of hatred and malice. |

| 439. De homine replegiando. | For replevying a man. |

9